Chakra Healing & Magick

Regina Chouza

CHAKRA HEALING & MAGICK

Copyright © 2016 REGINA CHOUZA

Editorial Supervision: Alexandra Brunais. Cover Design: Andrea Sarquis.

Illustrations: Shutterstock License

All rights reserved. No part of this publication may be reproduced by any mechanical, photographic or electronic process, or in the form of a phonographic recording; nor may it be stored in a retrieval system, transmitted or otherwise copied for public or private use other than for 'fair use' as brief quotations embodied in articles or reviews, without prior written permission of the author.

The moral rights of the author have been asserted.

DISCLAIMER

This book gives non-specific, general advice and should not be relied on as a substitute for proper medical care and consultation. Reiki, Energy Healing and meditation are complementary therapies. They are not intended to replace conventional medical care. If you have an acute or chronic disease you should consult a qualified health care professional.

While all suggested Self-Healing techniques are offered in good faith, the author and publisher accept no liability for damage of any nature resulting directly or indirectly from the application or use of information in this book, or from the failure to seek medical advice from a doctor.

Website: www.diaryofapsychichealer.com

All rights reserved.

ISBN: 978-1533449931

This book is dedicated to our Root Chakras. May we learn to ground ourselves, move beyond tribal thinking and live in harmony with Mother Nature.

CHAKRA HEALING & MAGICK

Table Of Contents

	Acknowledgements	i
	Introduction	Pg 1
Chapter 1	Laying the (Energetic) Foundations	Pg 3
Chapter 2	The Energy Body: A Blueprint for Healing	Pg 13
Chapter 3	Creative Healing Techniques	Pg 26
Chapter 4	Through the Chakra Rabbit Hole	Pg 34
Chapter 5	Awakening Your Inner Healer	Pg 53
Chapter 6	Psychic Development for Beginners	Pg 66
Chapter 7	Crystal Magick for Healing	Pg 83
Chapter 8	Magickal Co-Creation	Pg 100
Chapter 9	Conclusion	Pg 109
	Appendix I: Guided Meditations	*Pg 111*
	Appendix II: Chakra Quiz Follow Ups	*Pg 118*
	Appendix III: Suggested Reading List	*Pg 121*
	Appendix IV: Glossary of Terms	*Pg 122*

CHAKRA HEALING & MAGICK

Acknowledgments

I would like to thank my teachers at *The College of Psychic Studies* in London, where I studied Angel Intuition and psychic development for four years, and at the *School of Intuition & Healing*, where I gained my energy healing qualification. Especially Sue Allen, Natasha Wojnow, Julia Shepherd, Sharon Holmes and Amanda Roberts, from whom I have learned not only healing but what it means to have excellent teachers.

Also, I would like to express my gratitude to Alexandra Brunais, Vani Kurup, Gonzalo Gamboa Cavencia and Nancy Sunwolf for volunteering to sense check this Chakra Healing book. I couldn't have done it without such a lovely group of friends cheering me on along the way. Thank you!!!

Introduction

Welcome! Please settle yourself in for a creative journey through the Chakras. In these pages you will find a guide to healing yourself with creativity, intuition and (magickal) co-creation. You may be wondering what all of this means and if so, let's begin by defining energy healing – one of my passions – but what is it exactly, and what makes Healing so much fun?

You could say that Healing, especially the hands-on variety, is a complementary therapy that promotes mental, emotional and spiritual wellbeing, as well as relief from many stress-related health concerns.

Energy Healers channel a mix of universal and earth energies through their Heart and palm Chakras to the client's body and energy field – or in the case of self-healing, to their own bodies. We all have the ability to learn to heal and release stuck energy, emotions or anxiety. This type of debris can be created in our daily interactions. Let's say you had an argument at work and you found yourself exasperatingly tongue-tied. Not having the words to express yourself can leave a sense of frustration and even a constriction in your throat. I have been there a few times! Or maybe, you felt a pang in your stomach, where we tend to hold our personal power and test our boundaries. If this happens often, the energy builds and we may see chronic sore throats or even stomach aches. Energy healing aims to clear this from the physical, mental and emotional bodies. We can practice self-healing through meditation, or by channeling energy and sending it to different places in the body with our hands and with our intention.

For ease of reference, the healing and intuition techniques in this book rely on a basic understanding of the Chakra System and the Aura, which will be covered in Chapters 2 and 4. By working with the energy centers known as the Chakras, we can direct healing to specific themes in our lives, for example: spirituality, long-term vision, communication, personal power and confidence, appetite for life and our core foundations. Each of the Chakras and its corresponding Aura layer also relates to a different psychic ability, ranging from psychic visions and mental images (*clairvoyance*) to physical sensations (*clairsentience*), or the ability to sense other people's emotions. There are seven psychic abilities and together, they make up our intuition.

Finally, the last chapters are on magickal rituals for self-healing and manifesting. As opposed to stage magic, the magickal rituals in this book reflect the desire to create changes in ourselves and the world, with the use of focused energy, intention and tools such as candles, crystals and oracle cards. Magick can be used to manifest opportunities, such as landing a new job or renting a home, but we will focus primarily on crystal magick for self-healing. By transforming ourselves, we will be better placed to take advantage of the opportunities that the universe sends our way – often in response to our desires. I refer to this as magickal co-creation because we will combine energy healing and crystal magick with the abundance and the divine intelligence in the universe to manifest opportunities that lead to happiness. As you will see in the following chapters, once we have healed ourselves through the Chakras, our understanding of what we need to feel secure, happy, loved or fulfilled can change dramatically. From this place of empowerment and joy, living a blissful life becomes a real possibility. And with the intuition techniques in Chapter 6, we will become aware of the angels and spirit guides helping us on our journey.

While this book is designed to be a standalone resource, I would encourage you to follow my meditations on YouTube - and to subscribe to my blog, as I will answer questions through my weekly newsletter. Feel free to submit any questions or comments via Facebook or on email, below.

- Website: DiaryofaPsychicHealer.com
- YouTube: www.youtube.com/c/ReginaChouza
- Facebook: www.facebook.com/DiaryofaPsychicHealer
- Email: geena@diaryofapsychichealer.com

Chapter 1
Laying The (Energetic) Foundations

If there is one thing I have learned as a Healer, it is the value of learning to ground, clear and protect your personal space. This is especially important when we work with the Aura and the Chakras, because the more we flex our energy body, the more sensitive we become to our surroundings. We want to get a feel for our angels and guides when we are working intuitively, but if we are just as open in our daily lives, we may be overwhelmed by the energy or emotions from strangers on the street, the bus, etc.

This chapter will introduce the basics so that you can build your energy from the bottom up. Please get a feel for the different techniques. Experiment and decide for yourself what works and what doesn't. I would suggest one month on daily grounding, clearing and protecting before moving onto Chapter 2.

It is worth mentioning that many professional Healers could do with deeper grounding, myself included!

Step 1) Grounding: The All-Purpose Remedy

When my clients ask what they can do to get a grip on their lives, I tend to suggest grounding. It brings mental clarity by releasing any excess energy, stress, tension and fatigue into the Earth for cleansing and purification. So, if you are feeling scattered, overly excited or even light-headed; ground yourself. Tired? Ground yourself. Easily overwhelmed by crowds and by the sea of emotions and energies in the world?

Ground yourself.

It has been said that we are spiritual beings having a human existence and that we shouldn't forget that spiritual aspect. Our spiritual aspirations aside, we will always remain *human* and that messy emotional side is a big part of the equation. Our hopes, dreams and ambitions co-exist with our spiritual power in a human package that is subjected to the stresses of everyday life. There are bills to pay, relationships to help us evolve, kids to raise and all of this makes for dynamic and sometimes volatile energy.

We often need a moment to slow down, to connect with Mother Nature and let all of that energy run into the ground. Wouldn't it be wonderful if we could also draw on the nourishing and supportive energies in the Earth to stay motivated? This is what grounding does for us - it improves our connection to the Earth while providing an escape valve for messy emotions and superfluous energy. The epitome of renewable energy, we can release what we have used and draw on fresh earth energy for sustenance.

We will cover the Chakras in Chapters 2 and 4, but many of us are energetically inclined either to the upper "metaphysical" or the lower "manifesting" Chakras. The upper Chakras take our perception beyond the physical to the spiritual realms, while the lower Chakras receive that spiritual energy, anchoring it in the physical world where we can use its creative power to shape our lives. Ideally we would aim for balance; all the Chakras are equally important when it comes to healing. If you are usually in the moment, in tune with your body, and aware of your surroundings; then grounding may come naturally to you. If however, you are an empath or otherworldly minded, it's likely that grounding will be a challenge but the upside can be tremendous. Grounding makes it easier for us to feel safe in our bodies, to channel healing, and to receive timely, accurate and relevant messages from the spirit world.

Here are a few grounding techniques, please try them and see what works for you. Most of these rely on the notion that *energy follows thought* (or voice). When we tell our energy body to adjust, it obeys.

The simplest way to do this may be to use guided meditations, telling our energy and our unconscious that we want to ground ourselves and merge with the Earth. The secret is to say it out loud and to repeat the process often until it becomes a habit. In Appendix 1 you will find the scripts for some of my favorite meditations. Record yourself at your own pace - this is easier than ever with smartphones. I would also suggest the Flowerbed Meditation in Chapter 6 to ground yourself and unlock your intuition.

In the meantime, here are a few short visualizations to get you started:

Tree Roots: Visualize brown roots growing out of the bottoms of your feet, into the ground. Follow these roots with your mind's eye as they cut through layers of dirt, rock and concrete. Eventually they reach the center of the Earth, where you find a large crystal formation. Your roots wrap around this bright crystal, drawing on its energy for healing and renewal. Bring your attention back to the Earth's surface and your feet, while remaining conscious of the crystal at the center of the Earth. The roots are flexible, allowing you to walk while continually energizing you with crystalline energy.

Focus on Your Feet. Bring your attention to the soles of your feet and intend for your foot Chakras to open up ever so slightly. Count three breaths and turn your attention to your left foot. The left side is the receiving side. You are going draw earth energy into your body through this foot, letting it flow up the left leg. That energy crosses your hips and flows down your right leg into the ground. We can also draw earth energy up both legs and then release it into the ground by visualizing a grounding cord at the base of the spine, sinking deep into the ground. Repeat this process for two minutes, twice daily.

Breathing Meditation: Sit in silence for two minutes focusing on your breath. Breathe in love, and breathe out stress. Continue to breathe slowly, listening to your heartbeat and falling in sync with its rhythm. Our bodies are in tune with nature and by connecting with our breath, we can start to ground our energy and bring our attention back to the present moment.

A Walk In The Park: Spending time outdoors can be incredibly grounding, especially if we combine it with a meditation to activate the Earth Star Chakra – the lowermost energy center in the human energy field. Located 12-18 inches beneath our feet in the ground, we can activate the Earth Star Chakra to deepen our grounding while strengthening our relationship with Mother Earth. This also makes it easier for us to connect with crystals and with the plant and animal kingdom. Activate it by going for a walk in the park, near trees if possible, and visualize a green star coming to life beneath your feet. Focus on this feeling of oneness with nature and breathe slowly.

Guided meditations and visualization works well for me, but they do not suit everyone. If a person is especially ungrounded or not that visual to begin with, the following techniques may be more effective:

Wear Crystals for Grounding. Crystals come from the Earth and their energy is inherently grounding, but certain varieties go even deeper, such as Black Tourmaline or Red Jasper. The latter has calming energy and its color resonates with the Root Chakra, at the bottom of the spine.

Grounding Essences. There are plenty of vibrational remedies that can help us ground our energy by leveraging the stabilizing qualities of the plant kingdom. For example, the Bach Flower Remedy known as Clematis can help watery and intuitive types find solid ground again. Rock Rose can help the dreamy Piscean mind come back to reality, leaving endless mental scenarios on standby.

Get Physical: Yoga, Tai Chi, Pilates, breathing exercises and light stretching can help us reconnect with our physical bodies, grounding our energy in the process. Leg lifts and squats work wonders.

Do a Little Dance, stomp your feet, move your hips, or walk barefoot. If you enjoy drumming, find a shamanic dance class on YouTube and use the movement and music to connect with the Earth.

Concrete Boots or Sand. One of my teachers at the *School of Intuition & Healing* offered this as an alternative to roots. Sit or stand and visualize yourself in concrete boots, anchoring you to the floor.

My fellow blogger and healer, Justin Luria, has a fantastic website called *Healing for Grounding* that is dedicated to helping spiritual types ground their energy and embrace a messy human existence. He also runs the *School of Earth Medicine* in London. In Chapter 4, I explore grounding through the Chakras, including a guest post by Justin on traumas that can prevent us from grounding our energy or feeling safe in the world. In some cases, we may need deeper healing before achieving this level of grounding.

A Grounding Quiz: On a scale of 0-100%, how grounded do you feel? Ask your intuition before and after each session. Write down the first number that comes to mind. With time, we want to get to 85-100%

Step 2) Clear Your Energy

When we connect with Mother Earth, we feel protected and supported by her loving warmth. Now and then, however, we may absorb energy or emotions that make us feel uncomfortable, possibly the byproduct of a misunderstanding with a friend or a confrontation with a coworker. Our thoughts, emotions and interactions leave an imprint on our personal energy field (or Aura). We can release those sensations before they start to weigh us down. This can be done by clearing your personal energy field, your workspace or your bedroom, for a lighter environment. As Healers and Intuitives, regular energy clearing also makes for a clearer, faster channel. These are some of my favorite clearing techniques:

Wash your Hands. This is one of the most effective techniques for me, especially after healing sessions. It is not just any hand wash. Visualize white light or even a stream of water running through your whole body into the ground while you rinse your hands in cold water. This technique combines the intent to clear yourself with visualization and real H20, for our first magickal ritual of sorts.

A Shower of Light. If you are nowhere near a faucet and you still need to clear yourself quickly, take a few deep breaths, throw down your grounding roots and visualize a shower of light over your body. The key is to command that light to appear, so that it follows your intention, as opposed to imagining that it is there (the same goes for all of our visualizations). That light clears your energy field slowly, taking any and all particles with it as it continues to shower you with love and healing light.

Go for a Walk. This is a classic way to clear our energy; it is also where the expression "get some air" comes from. The human energy field can get bogged down with thoughts, confusion and debris, all of which cause blind spots in our thinking. When we go for a walk and "get some air" we connect with the spirit of the wind for a clearing on the mental level. The mind is ruled by the element of Air.

Flower Essence Sprays. There may be times when we need heavy duty clearing and no matter how focused our guided visualizations, and we can't seem to shake that icky feeling. This is when I turn to my trusted flower essences and sprays, which use vibrational healing to dissolve psychic debris. There are several brands; I prefer Alaskan Flower Essences, especially one called *Lighten Up*.

Blow Dry Your Hair. This is a quick fix if you are stuck on a problem that doesn't seem to have a solution. Thinking too much generates psychic debris around our Third Eye (thinking Chakra) and Crown (Divine Inspiration), which can bring on a mental fog that keeps us from seeing the answer. On occasion, I have picked up a hairdryer and "*blown*" away that debris using the "cool" setting.

Crystals. Similar to flower essences, crystals have unique vibrations and structures. We can work these patterns to our advantage. Amethyst crystals are said to transmute negative energy, replacing those feelings with a loving vibration. This violet stone works for simultaneous clearing and protection. Crystal Quartz can also be placed near the door to purify anyone who enters.

Clear Quartz Pendulums. We can also use pendulums to clear a room. Hold the pendulum in your hand. We charge it by visualizing light coming down from Heaven, pouring down through the crown of your head to your heart and down your arm to your palm. Ask that it clear, balance and heal the energy in the room. Hold the chain with your dominant hand, the pendulum pointing down, and ask it to begin. The pendulum will spin while it clears the energy and will stop when it's done.

Shake it Off: Learning to let things slide will go a long want to keep your energy clear. Did someone say something that rubbed you the wrong way? Does it feel like the moms at school are critical of your choices? In the words of the beautifully talented Taylor Swift, *Shake It Off*, and dance!

Go for a Swim: Water, fire and air are the cleansing agents in the universe, and what could be more appealing than taking a salt bath or going for a swim in the ocean? Salt water is quite cleansing.

Make a To-Do List: Often, it's the weight of our responsibilities that keep us up at night. Organizing yourself with a to-do list will help keep your mental body clear, increasing your ability to focus, get things done and of course, sleep at night. Keep a notepad by your bed and jot down stray thoughts. In the morning, highlight the bigger ones and tackle those first. You will breathe easier that day.

Burn Baby Burn: Now for another list, this time, one with all our regrets, fears, and frustrations. We can release that emotional energy by making a list and burning it safely, or even by tearing it up and flushing it down the toilet. Visualize that list going down the drain to fire at the center of the Earth.

These are just some of the techniques that we can adopt for space clearing. Please try them for yourself and see what feels right. You will know that it works when you feel light and carefree. Next we will learn basic energy shielding and protection techniques to keep our personal space clear, day in and day out.

Step 3) Shield Yourself with Love

Once we start on this journey of healing, intuition and magick, we have to practice energetic shielding. The boogieman is not out to get us. Rather, opening up increases our sensitivity. We can literally feel other people's physical symptoms. I saw this for myself when I had a bout of sciatica; my classmates at *The College of Psychic Studies* would double over in pain if they sat next to me. By learning to ground and shield our energy, we can check all of those unpleasant sensations at the door. Shielding also has the added plus of blocking messages and intrusions from random spiritual beings. You wouldn't give every last human your phone number – so why give the whole spirit world access to your energy?

The key here is trusting that you are safe and loved. We can use an endless variety of visualizations to shield our energy, but the moment we feel doubt, a window opens. In healing school, we learned that the best way to shield our energy is to ground ourselves in Mother Nature's loving, life-giving and cyclical energy. Surround yourself with a cloud of love and trust that no matter what happens, love has your back. That said, you could also experiment with shielding techniques. We can have fun with this step, and as a Healer, I have come to realize that we each have our energy shielding visualizations. Seeing them come to life (clairvoyantly) during a client session can be fun – to each his own creations!

Again, the following exercises rely on the theory that energy follows thought and that by visualizing a bubble of light, we do create it. Welcome to your first steps as a magician. These techniques lay the foundations for the rituals that we are going to learn later on in this book. Let's make the most of them!

Bubble of Light. Visualize a bubble of light around your body. You may want to use your grounding roots to draw crystalline energy up from the center of the center of the Earth, to the top of your head and let it fall like a cascade, covering you in protective earth energy from top to toe.

Violet Flame. Most of the tense energy in the environment is the result of stray thoughts (Air) and intense emotions (Water), both of which are consumed and transformed by the element of Fire. We can transmute this by intending for a violet flame to fill our hearts and purify our energy.

Hand Placements. Place your dominant hand over your Solar Plexus Chakra when you feel taxed. It is located in the upper abdomen, just below the spot where our left and right rib cages meet. This is the Chakra through which we experience power struggles with others, and shielding can help us.

Ground Yourself. Back to square one - grounding yourself in Mother Nature's loving energy is a simple and effective way to protect your energy. Let Mother Nature's warmth fill your Heart Chakra.

Be Like a Tree. Picture yourself an oak tree, with deep roots anchoring you to the ground. You have strength and resilience to weather storms. Your branches reach out to the sky for air and sunlight. Let the breeze clear your energy while you continue to ground yourself under the sun's watch.

Sleeping Bags. Protecting your energy before you go to sleep will make it easier for you to wake up refreshed. While they can't do us any physical harm, earthbound spirits can wake us up in the night. When this began to happen, I visualized myself in a navy blue sleeping bag before going to sleep.

Accessorize. Wear a protective crystal, for example, a Black Tourmaline pendant or an Amethyst bracelet. Many religions also have their own protective symbols. The key is to trust that you will be fully protected as your faith and belief in the symbol will give it power in your energy field.

Mirrors. In school we were advised not to use this because it can lead to an escalation of *energy tit for tats*, but it can also be helpful to visualize mirrors protecting you, front and back. Any unfriendly energy will be returned to sender. You could send that energy into the ground, instead.

Angels. Call on your Guardian Angel for guidance and on Archangel Michael, to keep you grounded, clear and safe.

Step 4) Putting It All Together

Now that we have learned each step, let's bring it together in one ritual:

Start by grounding yourself. For example, you may choose to visualize tree roots growing out of the bottoms of your feet into the ground. Use your mind's eye to see and feel these roots as they cut through layers of dirt, rock and lava before reaching that big beautiful Crystal.

A shower of white or silvery light washes through your body and your energy field, removing psychic debris and particles, as these flow to the center of the Earth for purification. That white light clears your energy field while replenishing it with a love of the highest and purest vibration.

Your guardian angel stands behind you with a fluffy white towel. Pat yourself dry before wrapping yourself in a luscious white, pink or violet robe. This robe covers your head, shielding you from the elements and reaches your toes. We can alternate by visualizing silk robes for protection, sleeping bags, or an astronaut suit - whatever makes you feel comfortable and safe.

The deeper your grounding, the easier it will be to channel energy healing, receive psychic insights and eventually work your magick by programming crystals and talismans for healing and good luck.

Chapter 2
The Energy Body: A Blueprint for Healing

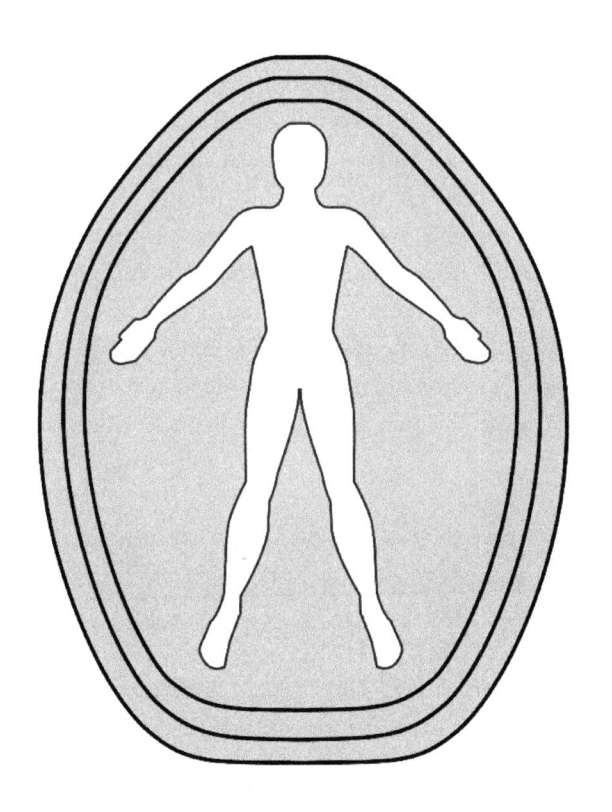

It would be easy to write an entire book on the Chakras and the Aura. For the purpose of this Chakra Healing book, I will cover the aspects needed to practice the techniques in the following chapters. These are designed to be simple enough for beginners. If you have any questions, please visit my Diary of a Psychic Healer Facebook Page. The more we meditate and connect with the subtle energy body, the easier it becomes for us to perceive it. Eventually we develop our own intuitive language; one that will help us receive messages from the body, in the form of physical sensations, temperature changes, etc; And from the Aura or the Chakras, as mental pictures, thoughts, sounds and feelings. Learning to interpret these images is fun and challenging, but worth it, if we are to find our unique path in life.

The Human Aura

The easiest way to understand the Aura is to imagine a bubble of light around your physical body. It is shaped like an egg and extends above your head, under your feet and out to your sides. This is what we refer to as the human energy field. On any given day, it will extend an arm's length in any direction, though it varies from person to person. If you have ever felt someone walk up behind you, they may have overstepped your auric boundary. The Aura is like a sponge; it absorbs the feelings associated with our day-to-day thoughts and interactions. Clearing the Aura can release tension from the physical, mental and emotional body. Otherwise, these feelings build until we start to feel overburdened. We can clear the Aura using the techniques in Chapter One. It also helps to shield our energy with violet light.

There are as many layers to the Aura as there are Chakras, with estimates ranging from seven to 12. For simplicity, I divide the Aura into four layers:

The physical Aura layer: This layer is closest to the body. It is often perceived as a red or brown color, an inch thick. Physical symptoms are often visible in this layer. During a healing session, I often scan the Aura with my hands. If I feel heat or tingly sensations close to a particular area, for example the knee, I send healing to this area and then smooth it out with my hands to release the energy. This is done in the Auric field without touching the body. After the session I will mention it to the client. If the tingling sensation was in the physical layer, they often comment on a recent bruise, accident or surgery.

The emotional Aura layer: One of my colleagues asked if a person's Aura changes color with their mood. Indeed, it does! The second layer holds our emotional reactions to life. It registers our mood as well as the feelings we absorb from others. An emotional situation generates energetic debris, which can accumulate here. This can affect the way we feel on a daily basis. A daily practice of Aura cleansing can reduce the emotional overload, especially if we are under a lot of stress, tension or dealing with emotional people in our lives. Please refer to the Aura Cleansing meditation in Appendix 1 for more information.

The mental Aura layer holds our thoughts, beliefs, memories and worries. If a person worries about the same things over and over again, it will show on this level. Over-analyzing a problem can muddle our thinking capabilities, which is why we "get some air" to clear our heads. That practice clears the mental Aura layer. Life makes sense when this layer is clear and the answers come to us naturally. I have also found that clients with busy mental layers (especially around the head) tend to complain of headaches. These are linked to repetitive thoughts and worries. Clearing the Aura can help relieve the headache. Thought forms and beliefs can also be cleared and released by thoroughly cleansing the mental Aura layer.

The spiritual Aura layer is linked to the Crown Chakra, and through it, to the Divine and to our soul memories. Having a strong Crown Chakra gives us clarity, purpose and a sense of direction. When that spiritual connection is weak our motivation fades. When the spiritual Aura and the Crown Chakra are clear, we are in tune with our spirit and our life purpose. When it is imbalanced by old and stuck energy, we lose our sense of direction and purpose. It is furthest from the physical body.

Meditation Tip: Take a minute to observe your breath. A white light fills the room, clearing the space around you. With your eyes closed, take your attention to your Aura. Imagine yourself stretching your arms as far as they can reach, above your head and to your sides. Your Aura fills with light. Intend for it to expand as you continue to breathe, releasing any stress or tension into the ground. Surround your Aura with violet light and let it expand. How does this feel? Get a sense of your surroundings and when you are done, bring your Aura back to its normal size. Send any intuitive sensations into the ground and shield yourself. With time, this technique will help you read rooms, people and situations simply by walking into them. Remember to ground, clear and protect your Aura when finished.

The Chakras

Often referred to as wheels of light, the Chakras regulate the flow of energy in the human body on a physical, emotional and mental level. The seven major Chakras each relate to a specific area of life, for example: physicality, creativity and passion, self-expression, experience of love, communication, vision and spirituality. When a Chakra is clear and active, that part of life unfolds with ease. We are aligned with the flow of life, ups and downs are easier to navigate. This alignment can be facilitated by a daily practice of meditation and Chakra balancing. For example, think of the last time you had a misunderstanding with a friend. The experience may have left you with an unpleasant aftertaste. That feeling corresponds to an imprint in your Aura, which serves as a reminder and an imbalance. This is what I refer to as energetic debris. It is generated by daily interactions, thoughts and feelings.

Over time, this energetic debris will accumulate until it clouds the Chakras and reduces the flow of energy. This is often referred to as a block, though imbalance is a more appropriate word. Chakras are rarely fully blocked. When a Chakra is out of balance, we start to feel stuck physically and emotionally. By clearing the Chakras we rid ourselves of that feeling and we also re-establish the flow of energy in the body. I like to think of the Chakras as the body's natural air conditioning system. When they are clear and connected, energy flows smoothly and freely. For example, a slow Sacral Chakra may diminish our experience of wealth. It becomes increasingly difficult to make ends meet. The challenge may be felt in any of the areas that are typically linked to the Sacral Chakra. We may feel aches and pains on a physical level as well, as the Chakras regulate the flow of life force energy to the body's organs and tissues.

We can send healing to the Chakras with guided meditations, or by channeling energy through our Heart and hands, and placing a palm on the Chakra being healed. We can also stimulate a Chakra by engaging in activities that relate to that energy center's issues. For example, the Sacral Chakra is related to creativity so drawing, painting or sculpting will stimulate it. Likewise, we can balance, clear and heal the Throat by singing, chanting or by writing. Self-Healing doesn't have to be a meditative experience either - we can engage in self-healing by enjoying a good laugh or even a game of charades.

The major Chakras can be found at the base of the spine, the navel, below the ribs, the heart, the throat, the forehead and the crown of the head. Each of the Chakras is associated with a color and a sphere of life.

The Seven Major Chakras

There are dozens of books on the Chakras and as part of my healing studies, I read quite a few. One that struck a cord was *The Seven Lies of the Human Race*, by Maria Veiga. As a healer and therapist, Maria maps out our psychological development stages as they relate to the Chakras. It is also one of the most relatable books on the subject - recounting the role that these energy centers play in our lives through the honest lens of the author's life, which has not been without its hardships and joys. I am pleased to include a guest post by Maria, who volunteered to share her unique perspective on the seven Chakras:

The following is an excerpt from *The Seven Lies of the Human Race*:

"Root Chakra (Red) – Trust

This is where life begins. The Root Chakra's energy is about surviving and having our first needs met. It is about the 'I,' the 'me.' It is the baby stage of life where we cry for food. Some of us cry and receive that nourishment. Some of us are given a bottle instead of the breast. Others are left hungry. Some learn to trust that their needs will be met, and others lack that trust from day one.

This energy is about feeling safe; it is about our instincts, basic impulses, fight or flight reactions, and the connection with our primitive self. It rules our connection to our communities, our tribe. Some of us may never feel safe, or we feel unsafe and have nowhere to run. Some of us learn to trust our instincts, and others may lack this survival skill because they were often told that they were wrong.

Sacral Chakra (Orange) – Relating

This is where we start relating, going from the 'I' to the 'me and you.' At first the world is about 'me', and I am discovering 'me'. My mum, the breast and the world is an extension of me. I do not know me so what I see must be me. That is why it is so important in infancy for a child to have a good enough mirror; someone who demonstrates the child is loved and valued.

But some of us don't have this: the mother may not be physically or emotionally available. We don't have that person to teach us that we are loved— no one to give us the healthy attention that we need. We begin to believe that attention comes with conditions. "If I do this, mom smiles. If I obey the rules, I get attention. Or, maybe, I don't obey the rules and I still get attention…" We start playing with control.

Solar Plexus Chakra (Yellow) – Self-Acceptance

This energy center is about self-acceptance, self-belief and self-esteem. It is where we develop a sense about things and situations: the gut feeling that so many of us lost touch with, or chose to ignore. Choice is the big theme with this energy center – recognizing the fact that we have a choice about everything we are involved in. How we choose to interpret the reality of situations is not only dependent on the 'reality' of that situation. This Chakra emphasizes our understanding of what is going on and how we take responsibility for it.

Heart Chakra (Green or Pink) – Heaven and Earth

This is the bridge, the connection between earth and heaven, between the three physical energy centers: Root, Sacral and Solar Plexus and the heavenly centers of the Throat, Brow (Third Eye) and Crown. We can connect with our soul/higher self in the Heart Chakra. It is the center of knowing, of intelligence beyond brain neurons or circuits and the home of divine intelligence.

The eternal energies of love and polarity come together here: heaven and earth, feminine and masculine, yin and yang, light and darkness, and good and evil. And it is where the whole becomes one. The Heart is like the sun at the center of our own solar system – the body. It is the center of existence, where everything else lives and feeds.

Throat Chakra (Light Blue) – Speaking our Truth

This energy center is about self-expression, free will, speaking our truth, and feeling heard. When it is connected to the Heart, we express our true self, our soul, and we speak the truth from a place of love and best intentions. Communicators and salespeople use the energy of this center, but not always for a positive outcome.

When you stand up for yourself at work, at home, within your family, at school or with your friends, this is the main energy you are using. Shy people have a weaker center and outspoken people a more energized one. It is often seen as pale blue in color.

Third Eye Chakra (Indigo Blue) – Universal Knowing

This energy center is concerned with the mind, thoughts, the questions and answers we find. More than this it is our connection also with the universal knowing (as distinct from the inner knowing of the Solar Plexus and all the influences we pick up there from others). The Third Eye, or Brow Chakra, is about consciousness, bringing divinity to our lives, guidance and help.

Imagination, visions, dreams, psychic perception and mediumship are experienced here (and are then expressed by the Throat Chakra, through speech and writing). Hence its name: the third eye. It is the 'eye' that allows us to see dimensions that are not visible to our normal sight, taking us beyond what is seen.

Crown Chakra (Violet) – Connection

This energy center stands for connection, aspiration, universal energy, life force, God, Divine energy. It is responsible for the flow of eternal knowing that sustains us. It facilitates the most powerful experiences of belonging, acceptance and self-worth that we can aspire to.

The Crown Chakra is where we understand that all of our earthly experiences, traumas, lessons and pain are a physical illusion, part of our experience in this world. We are wonderfully perfect and capable, with unlimited gifts and power beyond human understanding."

We also have small Chakras on the palms of our hands and the soles of our feet. These are especially important when it comes to healing, whether we are sensing energy in a crystal, grounding ourselves through the feet or directing energy with our hands. We also have what you might call transpersonal Chakras, which help us connect with the collective consciousness on Earth and in the universe. The Earth Star is located under our feet in the ground; it serves to anchor us in Mother Earth's loving energy so that we can sense tree spirits, flowers, crystals and even fairies.

There are at least three Chakras in the air directly over our heads, but these are best left alone until our foundations have been put in place.

A Basic Chakra Meditation

We are now ready to activate our Chakras! This process can be entertaining as well as healing. For me it has always been visual, so let's begin with a clairvoyant meditation that will guide us through the energy body. Our goal is to bring our conscious awareness into our Chakras and our Aura - so that we can work with these powerful energy centers to awaken our 6th sense and our natural healing abilities. These meditations are designed to be fun, so please enjoy yourself and let your imagination bring it to life. I would also encourage you to record these meditations and play them back, as your energy body and your unconscious recognize your voice. The goal is to bring your inner voice, your "speaking" voice and your conscious mind into a closer working relationship with your energy body. In time your energy body will recognize certain meditative cues, grounding, clearing and healing itself *on command.*

Step 1: Prepare Your Meditation Space

- Find a quiet place to sit comfortably. Keeping your feet on the ground and your back straight, please close your eyes. Ground yourself and get back in touch with your body by observing your breath.

- Next, we clear the meditation space by intending for a big white light to come down from the Heavens, through the roof, cleansing every last inch of the room. This light sweeps over curtains, desks, tables, and couches, reaching every last nook and cranny. The ceiling lifts off - carried away by this white light.

Step 2: The Chakra Journey Begins ...

- Ground yourself by visualizing tree roots growing out of the bottoms of your feet into the ground. They cut through layers of dirt and rock until they reach a crystal in the center of the Earth.

- The crystal changes colors to match your mood and your needs. Your roots wrap around the crystal. Stay with this image for a minute as your roots draw on its lovely crystalline energy.

- The crystal is full of light and liquid energy - you become that energy. This liquid invigorates your spirit as it makes its way up the roots, through the ground. Follow that energy as it flows into your physical body, traveling up your calves, over your knees to your Root Chakra at the base of the spine.

- You swirl through this red Chakra, clearing, healing and activating its beautiful energy. Keep an eye out for any energetic debris, possibly fears or doubts, and observe as they are washed away.

- This light enters the Sacral Chakra in an explosion of colors: reds, oranges, yellows, greens, blues - like melted crayons swirling in your center of creativity, passion and sacred sexuality. Let the colors melt away as your Sacral Chakra claims this space – a bright orange hue.

- The earthly, crystalline energy continues to rise as it reaches the Solar Plexus Chakra. This is where we hold our personality, our pride and our joy. You are surrounded by sunlight and yellow daffodils. These flowers stand tall as they bask in the warmth of the sun and its light.

- Take a deep breath and repeat: I am loved, respected and valued.

- Sit with these three energy centers as they continue to spin and grow a brighter red, orange and yellow. Your grounding roots are firmly in place.

- The crystalline energy rises to meet the Heart Chakra, the bridge between your physical body and your spiritual self. The Earth's energy comes to rest here as your Heart Chakra continues to grow brighter.

- Take your attention up through the sky, past the sun to a distant star in the atmosphere. This star transports you to the highest and purest source of light available in the universe.

- Connect with that Light - the source of all wisdom, power and love. You follow that beam of light, blending with its energy, as it travels through the universe back to your physical body. This light enters your body through the Crown Chakra at the top of your head where you may feel a prickly sensation.

- This divine light continues to flow down through your Brow Chakra, activating that whirling beam of indigo light in your forehead - front and back. The divine light shines on your life through your Brow, illuminating your path so that you can see yourself and your relationships clearly.

- Sit with this for a minute, before moving down to the Throat Chakra, where you can listen to your soul's guidance, your angels and your spirit guides. The Throat Chakra is an outlet for the creativity and passion in our Sacral Chakra. Sense this pale blue Chakra as it expands front and back, fully receptive.

- The light from that star reaches your Heart where it mixes with the Earth's crystalline energy. This creates sparks of light, filling your energy field with brightness. Your Aura grows stronger as this light continues to radiate through your seven Chakras, clearing, healing and balancing your personal space.

- Sit with this for a few minutes, letting your conscious mind observe the mix of earth and sky energy as it activates your Aura and heightens your awareness. Breathe in love, breathe out light, and repeat.

Step 3: Close Down Before You Go

- Take your attention to that distant light in the sky. Thank it for helping you and disconnect. Follow that beam of light through the atmosphere as it fades away slowly.

- Bring your attention to your Crown Chakra. It pulls in slowly, closing in on itself as it is desensitized to the spirit world. Your angels and guides can still reach you if needed.

- That beam of light travels down through your Brow, Throat, and Heart Chakras, as their external sensors switch off slowly. The Chakras return to their normal size, fitting snugly against your skin. Place a disc of light on each, front and back, desensitizing them to the spiritual world for now.

- Your Heart Chakra is just as bright as ever. We draw in its energy, front and back, and place a gold healing disc on either side to energize and protect it. You will always be surrounded by love.

- Repeat this step with the Solar Plexus and Sacral Chakras, placing a gold disc on either side. By shielding and desensitizing their energy, we are better able to reinforce our personal boundaries.

- The Root Chakra remains open to connect us with Mother Nature on a daily basis. We merely reduce its size, minimizing exposure and shielding it with white light. Check your grounding roots once more.

- The last step is to bring your Aura back to its regular size, just an arms length above, around and beneath your physical body. Surround yourself with violet light and know that you are protected.

It is important to end all of our meditations by closing down properly. This step makes it possible for us to go about our daily lives without interference from the spiritual or psychic worlds, and without feeling everyone else's emotions. The more we meditate, the more sensitive we become and the more attention we attract from the spiritual realms. We can end these meditations by placing an invisibility cloak around us, thereby neutralizing our personal vibrations, and shielding our energy and our space.

There are also plenty of Chakra Meditations that guide us through this colorful world with fewer creative detours. My personal favorite is a grounding, centering and "claiming your space" meditation by Elliot Jay Tanzer. You can find it on Amazon and iTunes. I have had it for five years and I still go through it at least once a week. My only suggestion would be to ground and protect your energy field at the end.

Meditation Tip: Ground your energy every day and run that crystalline energy up through your lower Chakras to your Heart, and down again. While it can be tempting to shoot for the starry skies, we will be able to accomplish more with that spiritual energy if we have first strengthened our lower 'manifesting' Chakras.

Chapter 3
Creative Healing Techniques

Exploring the Chakras can be an adventure if we let our imagination and our inner child roam free. In Chapter 4, I share a list of questions for each of the Chakras. Use them as meditation and self-healing prompts but keep in mind that we don't have to use words to express ourselves. You can also use music, arts and crafts, or even a blank canvas and your favorite acrylics to say what is in your heart. The soul communicates with our conscious minds through art; you will recognize the truth of what you are feeling by how it looks on the page. Don't worry about creating a masterpiece - the messier, the better!

Here are a few suggestions on how to channel your Chakra wisdom. Keep these in mind as you go through the individual Chakra sections and choose at least one or two techniques for each Chakra.

It might also be a good idea to put some of these creative healing techniques in practice before moving onto the next 'rabbit hole' section on the Chakras. Use these techniques to connect with your emotions and your energy intuitively, before focusing them on a sphere of life through one of your seven Chakras.

YouTube Sing-A-Long.

There is no quicker way to time travel than to listen to music from your past. Let's say we want to heal emotions or memories from a transitional period in our lives – we were leaving school, our parents might have gotten a divorce, or we may have dealt with the death of a loved one. All of these have the potential to be emotionally charged situations. We can send healing to those moments, releasing the imprint from our energy by listening to songs that were part of our vocabulary at the time. Open your browser, navigate to YouTube and type in a few keywords: "love songs + 1993" or "grunge 1990's" and see what comes up. Choose a song that you recognize and once it is playing, select the playlist. I like to sing along, letting the music take me back to those years as I confront and heal feelings that come up. It is OK to cry or even laugh yourself silly. Surround yourself with violet light to transmute that energy, and when you are ready, visualize those emotions running through your physical body into the ground.

If you like to dance, you may prefer to try freestyle dancing or even to stomp your feet on the ground. This is not a technique that I use often, but plenty of people love to dance. Start by grounding yourself by connecting to that beautiful crystal formation in the center of the Earth. Let its energy rise to meet you, preferably a bright red, orange or yellow color to stimulate your physical body. Imagine that color rising in swirls, moving with the beat of the Earth's heart. This energy flows through your body; it makes you want to tap your feet, move your shoulders and start to dance. Dance to the beat of your own drum, or if you would rather play an actual song, reach for the radio, your iPod or a favorite playlist. The purpose of this dance is to let your spirit move your body and act out your feelings with song and dance.

Some of us enjoy journaling. Another option would be to write about what comes up as you listen. We can do this by combining the YouTube sing-a-long with the following Automatic Writing technique.

Automatic Writing

One of my favorite healing techniques involves bringing your consciousness down to a quasi-hypnotic state and then asking questions of your soul, your angels and your physical body. This makes it easier for us to bypass the logical mind as we let our intuition speak to us through a pen and a piece of paper.

Find a quiet place to write and follow these simple steps:

- **Light a Candle**. Clear the room with a shower of light. Ground yourself by visualizing tree roots, clear yourself with another shower of light and activate your energy field by visualizing white light around your Aura, and intending for it to grow in size. Call on your guardian angel and your guides for guidance. Your angels and guides materialize in your Aura, where you can feel them.

- **Clear Your Mind:** We tend to have a lot on our plate. Start writing and don't stop until you have filled two full pages with everything on your mind. Finances, school, kids, laundry, shopping, etc.

- **Ask for Guidance**. Turn the page and write a phrase across the top. This could be "dear angels, please tell me what I need to hear right now" or to be more specific, "Please give me guidance on such and such topic. I lovingly put my trust and faith in your guidance. Thank you"

- **Write**. Count to 10 and start writing. It can help to identify a feeling and describe it – if what you feel was a color, what color would it be? Describe that color. This takes the pressure off us being able to receive a message. Your intuition will flow naturally from one color to the next.

- **Ask a New Question** and keep writing. Remember to thank your angels when you are done, before grounding, clearing and protecting your energy. Always extinguish candles by snuffing them out, rather than blowing them out. This shows consideration for the nature spirits that kept the flame alive during the meditation.

A Blank Canvas

Similar to the above, we can work with palettes and even crayons to channel a visual message. Color has wonderful healing qualities because we can pack so many emotions into one swirl of hues. Start with a blank canvas, connect with your emotions or with a particular Chakra and off you go. Don't worry about whether the colors match, or if the design is aesthetically pleasing. It is how we feel that matters, and how honestly we express the feeling. A preponderance of reds and oranges may highlight an issue with the Root or Sacral Chakra, the energy centers that anchor us in the physical and material world. Blues could hint at a message from the spiritual realms (Brow Chakra) or even a sea of emotions to explore. It is worth mentioning that specific colors can mean different things to different people. For me, gray is about resilience, like iron, whereas it might convey feelings of apathy and indifference to someone else.

Pay attention to the texture as well; patterns could indicate a need for structure. Ask yourself what you are drawn to explore, and how these shapes and colors enhance your general sense of wellbeing.

Chakra Mandalas

A mandala is a beautiful piece of artwork, full of patterns, colors and symbols – and one that we create as part of a meditative experience. It is a wonderful exercise, whether or not we create the mandala with a Chakra in mind. As a matter of fact, I don't know many people who do this, but it's a fantastic way to include color healing, creativity and meditation in our self-healing sessions. Louise Hay and Alberta Hutchinson published an *Affirmations Coloring Book* that works well for this purpose, as each mandala has an affirmation to go with it. We can link the affirmations with the Chakras, and use colors that stimulate and heal that Chakra. For example, affirmations about love relate to the Heart Chakra, and we can include pink and green in the mandala, dialing up these colors as we feel more love pouring into the mandala through the pencils, and into our energy field.

Affirmations about power or safety may include red (Root) and yellow (Solar Plexus). Repeat the affirmations out loud as you color in the mandala. As always, begin the healing meditation by activating your energy, and finish by shielding it.

The following is an example of a mandala. We can bring it to life with an affirmation from Louise's Hay's book, such as: "I breathe in love and I flow with life," a powerful one for trust (Heart Chakra). A recent discovery, Louise Hay's *Affirmations Coloring Book* is one of my favorite healing tools.

Coloring Books for Grown-Up Children

I honestly believe there is no better way to get in touch with your Inner Child, so grab a set of pencils and find yourself a coloring book. There are plenty of coloring books for grownups but those for children will do the trick just as well. If you can find a theme that was popular when you were a child even better, but that could be a tall order. Again, we are going to get creative with the colors, so that individual Chakras are highlighted. I also like to play with white spaces, leaving parts of the image blank until I am ready to begin work on a different Chakra. So for example, if we are looking to balance the Solar Plexus (personal power), we will reach for yellow and blue pencils. In this case we might use yellow to clear and heal the Solar Plexus, and blue for Brow Chakra where we hold beliefs about our personal power. This technique may require more imagination, but it is a helpful way to create a new world in your psyche.

Once again, begin by grounding yourself, protecting your space and then channel your emotions and energy through the crayons onto the page. Color outside the lines if you feel like it and ask yourself what that means for you – likewise, if you are craving order you may find yourself well within the lines. If you are using a coloring book that is for children, be creative with this technique, adding emotions and story lines for any characters in the cartoon. For example, if there is a young boy in the coloring book and he is sitting by a tree, how does he feel? The most important messages come with the scenarios that your imagination brings to life. Are these cartoon characters happy, sad, or bored? What is going on in their lives and how does it mirror your own reality? Coloring books for adults come with a variety of images, including flora, fauna, mandalas, landscapes and even themed Harry Potter or Lord of the Rings books. Choose a coloring book that speaks to your imagination and to the fantasy worlds that you are drawn to.

If you are lucky to find a Tarot coloring book you will have struck a gold mine, as the symbolism in tarot speaks to our subconscious in ways that a Disney or Transformers animation never will. One notable exception is Disney's Fantasia, first released in 1940. This animated film followed the path of a wizard's apprentice (Mickey Mouse) through many of the archetypes featured in the Tarot's Major Arcana cards.

With regards to color associations, we can highlight emotions with shades of blue and gray, thought with yellow, security with green and passion with red. There are 78 cards in a tarot deck; the ones you choose to color in first will shed light on the healing too. In Chapter 7 we will explore this in more detail.

Use Affirmations

You may have heard of Affirmations, words or phrases that we can repeat to boost confidence levels or to unlearn beliefs about ourselves. Often touted as a manifesting tool, affirmations are also great for self-healing. My approach to Affirmations was shaped by a tutorial that you can find on the popular psychic development blog, A State of Mind. The site belongs to Nathaniel, a fellow Healer and friend. In his post titled *Affirmations 101,* he points out the sometimes massive gap between the affirmations we choose and how we feel about the subject deep down. For example, we might affirm "I am a powerful, abundant and joyful person." But how do we feel about those qualities deep down? In this case, the way we feel about abundance, power or joy can create a feeling of discord. This may be the case if one of those qualities is notoriously absent from our lives. Or maybe we feel guilty about chasing wealth. These moments of discomfort uncover an important psychological block that keeps us from enjoying the comforts of an abundant life. Nathaniel suggests tackling both the affirmation and the belief, as follows:

- Repeat the affirmation 3, 5 or 10 times.
- Jot down any feelings, thoughts or emotions that come to you.

One of the first questions to ask yourself would be: Do I believe that abundance is rightfully mine? And what about love, joy, happiness, or good fortune? If not, where does this resistance come from? Was it something you learned as a child? Maybe it is based on previous experiences. Write down your feelings, explore the topic and let it go. You are going to come back to your affirmations daily for at least a few weeks. If you follow this process, you will start to peel back the layers that keep you from your desires. This is a simplified version to Nathaniel's technique.

Next, let's look at how we phrase the affirmations. I find that the most effective affirmations are the ones that we write for ourselves, based on our personal feelings, beliefs and desires. I have written a short phrase that we may adapt to meet our needs. It is based on some of the psychological blocks that I have encountered in my healing practice so far. Choose a quality that you would like to bring into your life, whether it is love, abundance, joy or health. Repeat this three times, morning and night:

I deserve love
I enjoy love
I give love

Three important parts: The first line tells our unconscious that we are good enough and we deserve this quality. With the second, we give ourselves permission to enjoy it. And finally, by bringing sharing into the equation, we trust that it (whatever it is) will never run out. We do not have to hoard or stockpile it. By sharing, we grease the wheels of life so that they keep turning for us. This generosity does have to be balanced. We share because we will always have enough, not because we do not deserve to keep it, or because others will like us more for it. This giving is balanced, compassionate, joyful and measured.

You might also combine several qualities in one phrase. For example: "I deserve happiness, I enjoy love and I share my good fortune with others." Try it out and remember; the most effective affirmations are the ones we write for ourselves. Please read Nathaniel's post for more on this technique: Affirmations 101: What Do You Need to Know About Using Them For Inner Growth. The post is available at his website: http://astateofmind.eu/

Chapter 4
Through The Chakra Rabbit Hole

Our deepest fear is not that we are inadequate. Our deepest fear is that we are powerful beyond measure. It is our light, not our darkness, that most frightens us –
Marianne Williamson

How would you live your life, if fear were not part of the equation? Whether it is fear of lack, failure, abandonment, change, loss, loneliness, or powerlessness; feelings of fear and the accompanying sadness or anger can slow down our Chakras. When this happens, the flow of energy to the corresponding sphere of life also slows down. So for example, if fear is affecting your Root or Sacral Chakras you may have dozens of ideas but little energy to put them into practice. A weak Throat Chakra makes it harder for us to communicate with loved ones, taking a toll on our relationships. The remedy should be simple enough: put your trust in God or the universe - but our human minds still cling to that fear and it is through gentle self-healing that we can loosen its irrational grip on our energy body.

We have already discussed the basic themes associated with each of the Chakras. In this chapter we will go deeper with journaling and meditation prompts. Answer these questions honestly, rating yourself for where you are and where you would like to be. The issues highlighted can be intense; which is why I suggest using art to express emotions that we may not be able to put into words. We also want to focus on laying the foundations and working our way up the metaphysical ladder. Please spend a good deal of time on the Root, Sacral and Solar Plexus Chakras before moving onto the Heart and the upper Chakras.

All the Chakras go through phases where they are wide open, a bit closed, or just right. Their energy is constantly changing and it is normal to sense a clear Chakra one week, and blotches days later. These apparent imperfections are no cause for concern; we can clear them with our daily self-healing tools.

The Root Chakra: Energy, Vitality and Belonging

The Root Chakra is about community, safety, tribal identity and survival. There wouldn't be billions of people alive today if the reproductive drive hadn't been wired into our brains. A healthy Root Chakra allows us to feel connected to our community and safe in this world. It gives us the grounding, energy and stamina to carry on despite external challenges. A healthy Root Chakra makes it possible for us to weather storms. It also triggers our fight or flight response and any adrenalin rushes. As well as grounding through the small Chakras on the soles of our feet, we can ground through the Root Chakra although in some cases, we may need to heal deeper issues and traumas before we can feel safe in our bodies. Unconscious fear can block attempts to ground our energy and connect with the physical body.

This kind of healing may need to be gentle, patient and guided by a healing professional. It is my pleasure to feature an article by Justin Luria of *The School of Earth Medicine.* Justin is a gifted healer who has worked extensively with wounding, showing care and respect for the process and of course, the Healee.

Inherited fears that inhibit grounding
By Justin Luria

"Doing things to become more grounded is a good idea, suitable for everyone. But if you've tried things to improve your grounding and they don't work, what then? What if you imagine grounding roots going down, but they curl back up? What if you spend time in nature, or eat more root vegetables (or dark chocolate, mmm!), or take up mindful exercise, and still you find it difficult to ground and be grounded? What does that mean, and what can you do about it?

Another way of asking that question is, what is it that gets in the way of grounding? And the short answer is, fear.

Fear is the emotion, the physiological and energetic reaction and state that makes it difficult for us to ground. If we have a generous amount of fear within ourselves (and it's ok if we do, we all have lots of emotions and feelings and energy inside us of all different kinds) then that underlying energy can get in the way of our grounding.

That fear says things like "The world is not safe" and "You are vulnerable" and "People are violent" and many other things. There may or may not be some objective truth in our fears, but mostly, they are the generalizations of our wounded inner child.

Where Does It Come From?

These deep fears - not phobias or fears about specific things, but the deep, mostly unconscious fear of life that lives in our body-mind-spirit system, have two main sources:

What happens to us in the womb, during birth, and when we are young children. The emotions and dispositions we inherit from our parents and ancestry.

Things like birth traumas or upsets when we are very young have a significant impact on our sense of safety in the world. And in particular, how safe or insecure, and how welcome or rejected we felt while in the womb has a great importance in how we form our feeling of being safe and welcome, or unsafe and alien, as children and adults.

But those experiences don't happen in a vacuum; they happen on top of our innate character (which is both biologically and spiritually derived) and on the psychological content - beliefs, emotional patterns, fears - we've inherited from our parents. If what we come in with is a latent fear of the world, perhaps due to a historical/ancestral pattern of trauma. Maybe our family was forced to flee the homeland, or there are unprocessed shocks from personal tragedies. All of this sets the stage for us to feel fear as a basic state, and not be able to ground easily.

Grounding is, above all, about feeling safe and welcome in your physical body, and on Earth.

How Was This Fear Created?

This runs deeper than the lessons and 'wisdom' taught from parent to child: "Don't talk to strangers, strangers are dangerous" "Be wary of men, they are prone to violence and aren't safe to be around" "Watch yourself, people will cheat you and take advantage of you" and so on.

It happens at a biological level, in the epigenetic expression of genes. Our physiological arousal - fight or flight or freeze response - transmits to our children through the activated or deactivated state of certain genes. We can come into the world physiologically equipped and prepared for stress and hardship, if that's what our mothers felt, or was active in them when they carried us.

If that biological priming is present for us AND we experience a trauma in the womb, during birth or as young children, that can be enough to teach us (in a very primitive and primordial way, as we are too young for rational thought when it happens) that life is not safe and dangerous.

That's the internal feeling and belief that gets in the way of grounding and makes it hard to grow roots. Our adult mind may think "Let's grow some roots", but the inner child and our subconscious trauma (which may be so deep that it's literally in our DNA) says "No way! Life isn't safe.". And the roots come back up, because the part of us that, if we didn't have the trauma or fear, would be chomping at the bit to greet life and the world, is scared to.

Healing for inherited trauma and belief systems is thus a hugely important part of any healing process, especially around grounding."

We can identify and heal the Root Chakra by working with a qualified therapist or by engaging with creative self-healing techniques, as laid out in Chapter 3. On a personal note, I have found natal astrology to be invaluable as we can pinpoint our ancestral line, including any strengths, weaknesses or fears, and work with crystals, meditation and journaling to slowly bring them into the light for healing.

The following quiz will help you flex your Root Chakra. There are no right or wrong answers. Turn to Appendix 2 if you are curious about why a question was included.

- How safe or comfortable do you feel in your physical body?
- Do you trust your body to alert you when something isn't right?
- Do you meditate, practice yoga or connect with your body often?
- Growing up, did you feel supported by teachers, parents, and family? What survival skills, if any, did you learn during childhood?
- How would you characterize your ties to your *current* community?
- What is your relationship with Mother Nature?
- Where are your car keys right now...?
- And your wallet?
- Did you have to stop and think about the last two questions?
- How do you feel, on a scale of 1 to 10, (1 = frazzled; 10 = solid)
- How would you describe intimacy vs. sex?
- Would you label either one as good or bad?
- Close your eyes and see RED.
- How does that feel?

Root Chakra Meditation Prompt:

Find a quiet place to sit and ground yourself. We are going to go on a journey through the halls of the Root Chakra. Visualize yourself walking into a museum with seven large doors in the lobby. The first on the left is bright red. You open the door and walk into your very own Root Chakra Exhibition, full of photographs, portraits, sculptures and even graffiti on the walls. Let your imagination bring these to life as you wander through the hall. The images register in your conscious mind and when the meditation ends you remember them easily. Make note of what you saw, especially any emotions or memories that surface. Is there anything that can be removed from this exhibit? Have any of these beliefs outlived their purpose? Surround them with light and watch as your unconscious dissolves that emotional charge.

There may be items that make us feel uncomfortable but that refuse to disappear. When this happens it's because we need to work through that item's imprint on our energy body. Choose one or two of the creative techniques above and use these to explore, express and release that memory from your body.

The Sacral Chakra: Expressing your Creative Self

The Sacral Chakra may be the best-kept secret in the "Manifest The Life of Your Dreams" industry. It is the energy center through which we give birth to our goals and dreams. Without a healthy Sacral Chakra and plenty of grounding in the physical world, affirmations and vision boards stay on a purely mental level. We can't eat mental pictures, no matter how precisely we imagine that vegetarian lasagna. A healthy Sacral Chakra makes it possible for us to make our dreams a reality, or tune into an alternate reality and bring it to life in the physical world. What does a healthy Sacral Chakra look like? It mirrors the passion, creativity, originality, and enthusiasm in our lives, whether it's a relationship, a creative project, or a job that we pour our energy into. The Sacral Chakra also rules the female reproductive system and pregnancies. A healthy Sacral Chakra makes for regular monthly cycles, which bring windows of opportunity, whether we use those to create a human life, or to give birth to an idea. These rhythms apply to men as well, if they are in touch with the Divine Feminine or with Mother Earth.

The following quiz will help you flex your Sacral Chakra. There are no right or wrong answers. Turn to Appendix 2 if you are curious about why a question was included.

- When was the last time you looked at the Moon?
- Was it a full moon, new moon - what is the difference?
- Think back to your favorite art project in childhood - what was it?
- Do you play a musical instrument and if not, would you like to?
- How do you feel when you hear the word *Jumanji*?
- What about The Lion King, Hook, or Peter Pan?
- True/False: The saddest thing about the movie Hook was the idea that Peter grew up?
- Close your eyes and imagine the four elements running across your face (Air, Earth, Water and Fire). How do these feel and which "comes to life" for you?
- Are you able to sense other people's emotions and physical pains?
- Do you look to personal relationships for validation?
- Let's say you spent an hour counseling a friend on her troubles - how are your energy levels?
- Do you tend to put on extra weight over your stomach?
- How easy is it for you to be emotional with others?
- Would you say your IQ or EQ (Emotional Intelligence) is higher?
- How passionately do you care about the world and the people in it?
- On a scale of 1-10: how do you feel about our furry friends?
- Are you energized by intimacy and emotional exchanges?
- Do you enjoy spending time with groups?

Sacral Chakra Meditation Prompt:

The Sacral Chakra rules our emotional interactions with others – we often put on weight to protect it. We can use our mind's eye to visualize the Sacral Chakra's size, shape and color. Three to five inches wide is "normal" for a Chakra. Use your Intention to make it bigger or smaller in social situations and see how you feel. If it's too wide, we risk sponging emotions off others. When it's closed, our interpersonal relationships can suffer. Maybe it tightens with certain people and relaxes with others? The purpose of this exercise is to become more aware of the Sacral Chakra and the role it plays in our lives. Be sure to ground, clear and shield your energy when you have found a comfortable "diameter" for this Chakra.

This also our most creative Chakra, as it's associated with the inner child. Please use at least three of the creative healing techniques from the previous chapter to explore this Chakra - and have fun with it!

The Solar Plexus: Stepping Into Your Power

In her breathtaking deck, Gaia Oracle Cards, Toni Carmine Salerno tells us that "the 'you' you think you are an actor, playing a part your soul has chosen" and that the real *'you'* is pure light and love. That actor can be found in the Solar Plexus Chakra, where we hold our sense of self, our ego, our personal affinities and of course, our personal power. This is the 'you' that longs to be seen, embraced and cherished and guess what – it is not that different from the 'real you' that is pure light. Healing can help us integrate our physical self with our cosmic or spiritual self. While the Solar Plexus Chakra is pure joy, it can accumulate debris and this is why we use healing to rid ourselves of fear, doubt, arrogance, tyranny, shyness, or beliefs that lower our self-esteem. Once all of that extraneous material has been stripped away, we are left with happiness. It is especially important to be compassionate with ourselves when dealing with Solar Plexus issues because we may believe that deep down, *we are* these flaws. Not true.

At the *School of Intuition and Healing*, we learned that the Solar Plexus is energetically paired with our thoughts through the Brow Chakra – including any unconscious beliefs about who we are. We constantly create an erroneous sense of self, which is why it's so important to keep an eye on our mental chatter.

The following quiz will help you flex your Solar Plexus. There are no right or wrong answers. Turn to Appendix 2 if you are curious about why a question was included.

- Picture yourself in a field of yellow flowers. How do you feel when you are surrounded by the color yellow? Are you filled with joy, overwhelmed or irritated? What color top are you wearing?
- You walk into a job interview and are asked to describe yourself in 15 words. Make a list and review it when you are done. Ask yourself if you decided to omit anything major. Why?
- Think back to High School - what role did you play? For example, if you were an athlete did this come naturally to you, or did you join the team to fit in? Was this the first "acting role" in your life?
- Is there a situation in your life that you would like to change?
- If so, what is holding you back?
- You are overworked, late to pick up the kids and the in-laws are coming over for dinner at 6 pm. A friend calls with a big favor to ask. Do you take the detour to help her out?
- You are at the supermarket and see a woman talking loudly on her cellphone. She cuts in line ahead of a six-year-old child, edging her way to the front. How do you respond (if at all)?
- What comes to mind when you hear that: *he or she is so spiritual?*
- Someone who looks out for herself is: a) smart, b) selfish c) normal
- How do you feel about people we might call bullies?
- What do you like most/least about yourself?
- What qualities do you most admire in a person?
- What or *who* rubs you the wrong way?
- On a scale of 1-10: how often do you get mad?

Solar Plexus Meditation Prompt:

Rather than a visual meditation, we are going to use physical posturing to boost our confidence levels. This has a direct effect on the Solar Plexus so please make a note of how you feel as you go through them. Confidence is a determining factor in our self-esteem and how others respond to us. High confidence levels make it easier for us to take risks, or to have a healthy sense of self-worth. Let's say you want to ask for a promotion but the boss makes you nervous. Power poses can help us boost our confidence levels and mental state, as outlined by social psychologist Amy Cuddy in her TedTalk: *Your Body Language Shapes Who You Are*. (Which can be viewed online at www.Ted.com) Before going into negotiate the raise, you could take two minutes to practice these poses out of sight, and confront the boss when you are ready. Of course, we can also practice these daily to slowly bolster our confidence levels and change our outlook on life.

The Heart Chakra:
Giving and Receiving with Grace

The Heart Chakra is primarily known as the giver and receiver of love but it does much more than that. As the bridge between our lower manifesting and upper metaphysical Chakras, a healthy and open Heart Chakra receives intuitive messages from the Earth and the spirit world, translating these messages simultaneously. When the Heart is functioning properly, we know that we are safe and loved because we can feel that love in ourselves and the world. Our sense of direction is also sharper as the Heart indicates which path to choose. If this weren't enough a healthy, open Heart Chakra also opens doors for us to perceive and accept opportunities as they arise. The Heart is the gateway for abundance.

There is such a thing as too much Heart, and I often see it in client sessions. When the Heart is overextended, we give too much of ourselves. So much that we risk depleting our energy and making ourselves sick in the process. Kindness and compassion are overemphasized as we show kindness to everyone but ourselves. This takes a toll on our self-worth because our actions tell our unconscious mind that our own needs are less important. The Heart is about giving and receiving, so the flow of energy going out (compassion, kindness, sharing) has to equal that coming in (self-care, asking for help).

On the flip side, when the Heart Chakra is closed we put up walls and this can keep love, friendship, happiness and even opportunities out of our line of vision. These blind spots can be selective, blocking money but not love or health. When this happens it is because of the judgment placed on the aspect being blocked. We might tell ourselves that "spiritual" folks don't idolize money, status or recognition. Or maybe our sense of self-worth is wrapped up in the quality being blocked, and we still need to heal that association. The Chakras don't operate in isolation, so for example, self-worth can be addressed by healing it on an emotional level through the Sacral Chakra, looking at conditioning from our families (Root Chakra), and any beliefs held in the Brow (Thoughts) and Solar Plexus Chakra (fake sense of self).

The following quiz will help you flex your Heart Chakra. There are no right or wrong answers. Turn to Appendix 2 if you are curious about why a question was included.

- Close your eyes and picture two flowers, one in each hand. Which is healthier? Which needs attention and care? The left side represents what we receive from others; the right side is what we give to others. When they are balanced, we give and receive equally.
- How do you define wealth, prosperity and abundance?
- What do you love most about yourself? What do you love least?
- True/False: My body is a channel for love and healing.
- What qualities do I admire most in a friend?
- When is the last time you sat and connected with nature?
- When was the last time you cried and how did it make you feel?
- Stand in front of a mirror and look at your face. What do you see?
- True/False: Love is kind, love is compassionate, love is patient.
- True/False: Self-love is kind, compassionate, patient, and forgiving.
- True/False: I am my own best friend

Heart Chakra Meditation Prompt:

Close your eyes and picture a flower in front of you. It is facing your Heart Chakra and its roots are beneath your feet. Bring it to life in your mind: what color, size and shape? Is it closed, beginning to bud or fully open? What does this flower need to grow? Maybe water, light or do we need to clear weeds?

Write about this image and what it means for you. For example, if the flower is blooming and full of life, how does that reflect on your Heart Chakra? What of a slightly closed bud? Or one that is dry, or needs pruning? The image is a visual metaphor for how we care for our Heart Chakra and how we can improve on that self-care and self-love.

Throat Chakra:
Speaking Your Truth

The Throat Chakra is about courage and communication. This energy center makes it possible for us to tell the world, "*This is who I am, what I stand for.*" Archangel Michael, the angel of courage, strength, protection and all kinds of battles is associated with the Throat. It takes courage to open up emotionally and share our feelings, or to voice an unpopular opinion. Listening to constructive criticism can also put us in a vulnerable place, but without it, we may not be able to grow. The Throat Chakra also makes it possible for us to listen to our spirit guides, angels and Higher Self. It builds on the foundations of Root, Sacral, Solar Plexus Chakras, as well as the unconditional love of the Heart, making it safer for us to open up.

If the Throat is too far open we can say hurtful things without considering the effect that our words have on others, justifying this as honesty. If it's too tight, we can create a barrier between our inner selves and the rest of the world. Angry outbursts can also be a symptom of an unhealthy Throat Chakra as the Throat is energetically paired with the Sacral Chakra's emotional health. This is an essential outlet; it's important to clear, heal and balance it regularly. Activating the Throat Chakra can also involve finding the communication style we feel most comfortable with, for example, dialogue, journaling, singing, etc.

The following quiz will help you flex your Throat Chakra. There are no right or wrong answers. Turn to Appendix 2 if you are curious about why a question was included.

- On a scale of 1-10, how would you rate your communication skills?
- Do you find it easier to process ideas silently, or to think out loud?
- When relaxing to music, do you sing along to the lyrics or the tune?
- Do you find it easier to speak from the Heart, or to think about what you want to say and formulate your thoughts first?
- We all have an inner voice that appears when we read, but we rarely think about it. Bring that voice down to your Throat Chakra, energetically, and keep reading this book to yourself, silently.

- Practice reading (silently) with a booming voice, then with a singing voice, a whisper, a child's voice, a politicians, a French accent, etc. Do you find it easy to manipulate this inner voice?
- Let's say you are in a debate and your opponent is speaking. You will have to respond to his argument in a few minutes. Are you listening attentively, or are you planning your response instead?
- Now, let's say you are in a row with your significant other – are you able to listen and respond?
- You have a brilliant idea and can't wait to get started. Your friends and family try to talk you out of it. Do you listen to "reason" or not at all? Is there resistance, and if so, where does it come from?
- As a child, did you have frequent ear and throat problems?
- Are you swayed by rational or emotional arguments - or both?
- Do you suffer from phantom pains?
- Do you yell "shotgun" in life, or let others take the front seat?
- True/False: We all fudge the truth with others to a certain degree.
- How spontaneously do you express your emotions?
- Are you honest with yourself?

Throat Chakra Meditation Prompt:

Part of our personal evolution involves looking inward and identifying character traits that need to be healed and released. When the Throat Chakra listens to the Heart's truth and unconditional love as well as the Brow's objectivity, we are better placed to love ourselves unconditionally. In a roundabout way, this acceptance gives us the strength to listen to healthy criticism and change self-defeating behaviors.

The following technique can strengthen the communication between the Throat and the Heart Chakras:

- Light a candle and protect yourself with a bubble of light.
- Visualize a grounding cord going from your Heart to the center of the Earth. Draw on the Earth's energy to activate your Root, Sacral & Solar Plexus Chakras by letting it flow through each of them.

- We have many compartments in our Heart Chakra. Ask your guardian angel to surround you with love as you travel to the deepest corners of your emotional Heart. What do you see?
- Ask your Angels to give you a memory. It could be an image, a scent, a sound. Surround that image with light and write about how it has influenced your life. Are there any emotions attached to it?
- If you could go back and change what happened, what would you say to your younger self?
- How has this experience influenced you – are there any emotions or beliefs that can be released?
- Use this to visual write a more authentic "you" into your life story.

Journaling strengthens the connection between our emotions, our intuition and the Throat Chakra. We can record ourselves and speak if that is easier. It is not necessary to re-read or listen to this afterwards. Rather, the process helps us learn to speak and write about hesitation, without mental filters. Write an affirmation based on this more authentic you.

The Brow Chakra: Imagination, Clairvoyance and Clarity

The Brow Chakra is where we hold our thoughts, beliefs, and critical thinking skills. It is also where we access our clairvoyance, imagination and visual creativity. The more fiction we read, the sharper our mind's eye becomes. If our energy is grounded through the Earth Star Chakra, we may begin to see nature spirits such as fairies, centaurs, gnomes and tree spirits. The funny thing about the Brow Chakra is that visions often appear when we know they are possible – beliefs can block and unblock our clairvoyance, as I discovered in my very first psychic development class. Our teacher had us close our eyes and imagine that we were traveling to visit our classmate's home. She led us through a meditation, asking us how many rooms it had, how it was decorated, was it an apartment or a house, etc. When the meditation was over we described our visions to each other. As a beginner, the images in my mind came and went like a scene from Kate Winslet's *Eternal Sunshine of a Spotless Mind*, but I still managed to pinpoint a few elements. What blew my mind and opened my eyes to the possibilities was my classmate's description of my own flat, including the never-ending corridor with 28 doors before mine.

Since then I have always approached clairvoyance empirically, testing myself, checking my answers and asking my intuition for more images. That same teacher told us to make a list of three things we got right and to save anything we didn't understand for later. It would make sense eventually.

On a more practical level, the Brow Chakra also makes it possible for us to see our lives with compassion and with symbolic sight. Its detachment and objectivity can point to emotional causes for physical illnesses, as well as patterns in the types of lovers and friends we attract. We can also ask our intuition to point out errors in judgment that lead to rough patterns. Epiphanies are more common when the Brow and Crown Chakras are healthy and balanced. Chakra clearing meditations are particularly useful.

The following quiz will help you flex your Brow Chakra. There are no right or wrong answers. Turn to Appendix 2 if you are curious about why a question was included.

- We all hold beliefs that color the way we view the world. Beliefs like "all teenagers are immature" or "women are only interested in money" color the way we approach life and relationships. The notion that "the universe has your back" reduces stress, while believing that "we need divine intervention" may diminish our personal power and conviction in the face of challenges. We can spot these beliefs by looking at how different people approach and react to the world. Think of two people that you admire and ask yourself how they would react to a situation that you now face. How is their reaction different from yours, and what may be causing that difference? Can you spot a subconscious belief?
- Business students learn to do SWOT analyses: looking at an individual's strengths and weaknesses as well as potential opportunities in the market. Let's leverage this tool in our own lives. What changes would you like to make, and can you work with your strengths and weaknesses to achieve that?
- When challenged, do you respond emotionally or rationally?

- Your friend comes to you with a problem in her relationship. Do you let yourself become wrapped up her emotional turmoil - or are you able to distance yourself and offer objective advice?
- One of your coworkers comes to you with a bold idea. Is your first reaction to think "that is not possible, we can't pull it off" or do you help them think of ways to make it work?
- On a scale of 1-10, how introspective are you? How rational?
- On a scale of 1-10, how forgiving and merciful are you in business & personal relationships?
- Would you rather read a fiction book and create its world in your imagination, or would see it in the theater on the big screen?
- Try one of the meditations in Appendix 1. Make a note of your impressions.

Brow Chakra Meditation Prompt:

Option 1: Silent Movies and Theatre

In the following chapters we will work with tarot to access our intuition. Reading oracle cards becomes easier when we can look at the images and work out a story intuitively. Practice by watching cartoons or TV with the sound off and paying attention to the character's visual cues: the expression on their face, their posture and body language. If you are able to find scenes from a play on YouTube, this will be even more apparent as theater actors tend to rely on body language more than facial expressions. Observe the scenes, with the sound switched off, and let your intuition and imagination fill in the blanks. It does not matter if you are able to guess the plot line. The point is to practice reading these scenes visually.

Option 2: The Secret Language of Tarot

Find a Rider-Waite Tarot deck – the original is a good option – and separate the cards into five stacks. In one pile we have all of the Major Arcana, beginning with the Fool and the High Priestess and ending with the World. We will put these to one side and come back to them in a few weeks. The other four stacks hold the suits of Wands, Cups, Pentacles and

Swords. Each of these suits tells a story, one that we can decipher by studying each progressive card as though it were a scene in a movie. The Ace of Wands, for example, is a new beginning on the creative plane, the 2 of Wands is when those ideas take shape and so on, as we follow the hero through his journey through to the 10 of Wands. The court cards – Page, Queen, Knight, and King – are characters that come along to help him on his journey, to inspire the hero.

Lay out the suit of Wands from Ace through to the 10 of Wands and study them carefully. If this were a children's book with pictures and no words, what would you know from looking at the cards? Pay attention to the pictures, to your feelings and to the vibe you get from these cards. It's OK to make up the story as you go along – the task here is to develop your visual creativity and story telling skills. Once you have become familiar with all fourteen cards, shuffle them and pull three at a time to create a unique plot line. What happens in scenes one and two, and how is this resolved in the third card? Like life, we may be left with happy or sad endings, or perhaps with no real ending at all as this isn't a movie.

The task is to develop our intuitive sight so that in the future when we ask a question, our intuition can pop an image into our mind to give us an answer. By developing our own understanding of the cards we also develop a unique language – one that can also unlock our unconscious. Only after we have gotten to know the cards own our own terms, will we turn to the 'guide books' for the official meanings. Please begin by studying the Suit of Wands and move onto the other three when you are ready. In Chapter 7 - Crystal Magick for Healing - we will use our knowledge of the Minor Arcana to heal the unconscious through the Aura, releasing physical, emotional, mental and spiritual baggage with meditative rituals.

If you would rather not use the traditional Rider-Waite, find a deck that is based on the same structure with 4 Minor Arcana suits and 22 cards in the Major Arcana. (*The Wizard's Tarot* by Corrine Kenner is fantastic).

The Crown Chakra:
The Gateway to Our Intuition

The Crown Chakra is our connection to source, to God and the universe. Insights from the Crown Chakra flow through our Brow Chakra where they create images, through our Throats where we hear an "inner voice" or a whisper, and to our Heart Chakra where we know the answer. This Chakra also brings us one step closer to our soul's plan. A healthy and active Crown Chakra makes it easier for us to receive guidance from our angels, so it can be tempting to start our journey here, but it is important to build your energy from the ground up. In the meantime, we can ask questions and turn to angel cards, runes, tarot or other oracles for divine guidance. Our spiritual team is there, always ready to help us.

The following quiz will help you flex your Crown Chakra. There are no right or wrong answers. Turn to Appendix 2 if you are curious about why a question was included.

- Do you ever wonder why you are here on Earth?
- Have you connected with Archangel Uriel to ask for advice?
- Do you feel guided and supported by the universe?
- Have you found soul sisters and brothers in your friendship circle?
- Does everything happens for a reason?
- True/False: Spiritual willpower can remove the biggest obstacles.
- True/False: When I trust God and myself, my life flows with ease.
- True/False: My intuition answers all questions, big and small.
- True/False: We are all God's children and fellow co-creators.
- True/False: I am more than my physical body and personality.

Crown Chakra Meditation Prompt:

It seems like everyone wants to meet their angel and find out their name. Why wouldn't we be excited to make their acquaintance? Not only do they have lovely ethereal energy, but they do so much for us! By getting to know our angels we make it easier for their guidance to cut through the noise of our daily lives. We can do this with a simple meditation to strengthen that 7th Chakra connection. Have your angel join you for a friendly chat, grab yourself a cup of tea and find a place where you will not be disturbed. Follow this meditation to ground yourself, clear the air and sense your angel's radiant energy:

- Sit down, close your eyes and listen to your heartbeat.
- Visualize a breath of fresh air sweeping through your body from head to toe and let it empty into the ground beneath your feet. Expand your Aura and place a bubble of protective, violet light around your body, activating the spiritual Aura layer. Your angel can help with this.
- Ask your Guardian Angel to make their presence known. You may sense a color, a vibration or a scent. Take a few minutes to familiarize yourself with your Guardian Angel's vibration.
- Talk to your angel. Is there something you need help with? Quiet your mind and pay attention to any thoughts, feelings or impressions. Keep a piece of paper nearby to jot down impressions.
- Thank them for this chat and end the meditation by visualizing grounding roots out of the soles of your feet, clearing yourself with a shower of light and shielding your energy with violet light.

Do this once a week and soon you will recognize your angel's energy when you are out and about. They may interrupt with a friendly message or a timely warning. We can also ask our Guardian Angel to raise our vibration so we can sense other spiritual beings like the Archangels or Mother Mary.

Chapter 5
Awakening Your Inner Healer

Energy Healers draw on the healing energy in the universe, channeling it through their bodies and out their palm Chakras to the person receiving the healing – or in the case of self-healing, to themselves. Professional healers will have dedicated months or years to practice, building their energy fields before working with clients, allowing for a constant stream of healing energy. While there are advantages to seeing a professional Healer, we can also learn to channel healing for ourselves, directing that energy to different parts of our lives through the Chakras. So for example, if you want to improve your relationship with your mother, you may choose to send healing to that relationship by focusing on your Heart (unconditional love), your Solar Plexus (power struggles) or your Sacral Chakra (emotional exchanges). The more we practice self-healing, the steadier and smoother the flow of energy in the body becomes.

In this chapter I cover the basics so that you can heal yourself or others at home. I also would encourage you to sign up for a Reiki class or an energy healing workshop. If you cannot find one in your immediate surroundings, I offer live, online self-healing classes and webinars every month. Channeling is simple, but managing our energy levels takes practice. We need to leave our emotions, fears and wishes to one side. Otherwise we may burn ourselves out. A good way to avoid this is to call on angelic energy for help. Let the angels heal through you, and focus on holding the space for the Healee during the session.

Healing With The Angels

If you have read my blog, Diary of a Psychic Healer, you may have noticed that I enjoy working with angels. They are grounding, loving and supportive. We can ask for help with any kind of healing and they are more than happy to step in. They can fill our hearts with love, forgiveness, and strength. We all have guardian angels at our beckon call. But we can also work with the Archangels for deeper emotional healing. Archangel Raphael, in particular, specializes in the healing of children, animals, the planet and also adults. I find his energy to be grounding and comforting, especially on an emotional level. Sometimes it is easy to feel his presence as warmth in the Heart, a tingle on your face or even a green flash in your mind's eye. He shows up when called, so sit quietly and wait for his energy to surround you. A regular practice of meditation will make it easier to sense his energy. This can be as simple as observing your breath for a few minutes every day and letting the world fade into the background.

Many Healers draw on angelic energy during their sessions. Raphael can also step in when we undergo medical care. I often call on him if I am going to the dentist or to a doctor's appointment, asking him to guide the dentist's hand, heart and vision during the appointment. When I have family or friends going into surgery I do the same. The goal is to help the medical team be at their sharpest and most intuitive. I trust that Archangel Raphael is there and I let him do his job. The trick is to ask for his help and then hand the problem over to him. At that moment we need to make a conscious decision to trust Raphael and the medical team to take over. Stop worrying and trust that the angels will look after your best interests (which they will always do!), which may result in emotional, mental or spiritual healing.

In the next section I will take you through a few simple steps to channel Healing Energy. These are meant to help beginners through the healing process. I have included angelic healing, so that as novice healers, you can pass the responsibility for the healing session over to Archangel Raphael. This allows novice healers to detach from the outcome and act as a channel. In this book I ask Archangel Raphael for help. It is also possible to call on Jesus, Lord Ganesh, Kwan Yin or any other spiritual figure. This is still energy healing because the intent is to clear the Aura and the Chakras with energy. If you would prefer to channel healing without involving these spiritual figures, please use your intent to channel pure white, pink or clear light. Set your intent on channeling light of the highest vibration.

Exercise 1: Running Energy Through Your Body

We are going to start by running earth energy through the body and noticing how it feels. This also gives us the necessary foundations to channel universal light and healing without toppling over. Think of a skyscraper and how these buildings need deep foundations to achieve their impressive heights. Just like a tall building or a tree, we can access higher and stronger streams of energy if we are well grounded.

- Sit with your eyes closed and your feet on the ground. Bring your attention to the soles of your feet and intend for the Chakras there to open up ever so slightly. Continue to breathe slowly.
- You are now going to visualize two grounding chords dropping into the ground, from either foot. These anchor you to the ground while providing a steady stream of earth energy.
- Draw earth energy up your left leg, over your hips and down your right leg. Repeat this several times. This grounds your energy and activates your Root Chakra for increased vitality.
- When you are ready to move on, bring that earth energy up through your left side, to your shoulder, across your collarbone and down your right side into the ground.
- Continue circulating this earth energy through your body, your Heart and your legs.

Once this feels completely natural, repeat this with a third grounding cord going down from the bottom of your spine, into the ground. Bring that warm energy up your legs, through your body and then down this third grounding cord into the ground. Let the energy circulate freely, with the grounding cords going deeper and deeper each time. Your foundations grow deeper with each breath.

If we haven't made an effort to really ground ourselves in our daily lives, now is the time!

Exercise 2: Activating Your Palm Chakras

In this second exercise, we continue to work with Earth energy while also reaching for the stars and the Heavens. It is the mix of earth and universal energies that give our healings their power. We are going to draw on both, bring them into our Hearts and to our hands as follows:

I find that this kind of meditation works well if we record ourselves and play it back. We are telling the energy body what to do and it responds best to our (familiar) voice.

1) Ground Yourself. Visualize tree roots growing out of the bottoms of your feet, deep into the ground. These wrap around a beautiful crystal – let your intuition give you the color. Draw on that crystal's warm healing energy and bring up your roots, your legs and core to your Heart. Feel this warm earth energy in your Heart and stay with it for at least 30 seconds.

2) Attune to Divine Light. Take your attention up through the stratosphere to a distant star. This star acts as a portal of energy, transporting to you to the highest and purest source of light in Heaven. Connect with that light and bring it back, through space, to your physical body. That light travels down your Crown Chakra, past your Brow and your Throat to your Heart.

3) Entering the Heart Space. The earth and universal energies mix freely in your Heart Chakra, creating sparks of light, color and healing energy. The energy continues to build as your healing power activates, spinning gloriously. This energy and light fill you with warmth and healing love.

4) Activate Your Palm Chakras. Soon this whirling light and love overflows from your Heart, down your arms to your hands where it activates the Chakras on the palms of your hands. Sit with this clairvoyant image for a minute, intending for that steady stream of energy to flow through your hands. Turn your palms inward so that the energy flows towards your body.

5) Feel the Energy. Now hold your hands in front of your body, with your palms facing each other. Visualize a sphere of light between your hands.

This ball of light grows brighter and brighter as it fills with healing light and energy. Bring your hands closer together so that you can feel it, then further apart when the pressure starts to build. Play with this for a few minutes, bringing your hands closer together each time.

6) Closing Down. Take your attention back to that distant source of light and disconnect, thanking it for its healing energy. Bring your attention back to your Crown Chakra and visualize it back at its normal size, protected by a violet flower. Your Brow Chakra switches off, front and back, protected by an indigo flower on both sides. Take your attention down to your Throat Chakra and let it switch off, protected by a sky blue flower, front and back. We then place a pink flower on the Heart Chakra, front and back.

Your Solar Plexus returns to its normal size and you shield it with thick gold plates, front and back. This is the energy center through which we have power struggles with others so it always helps to give it extra shielding. We then bring our attention down to our Sacral Chakra, protecting it with an orange flower, front and back. Finally, the Root Chakra stays open, if just a little bit narrower to reduce exposure.

Shield your Root Chakra with white light and keep your grounding cords in place, deep in the Earth. We finish by running a shower of violet light through the Aura and shielding ourselves with violet light.

Healing Tip!

You may have noticed that we spent quite a bit of time opening up (activating our energy field) and then closing down again, when we disconnected from that light. These steps, along with regular grounding, clearing and protecting will make it possible for you to channel powerful energy without becoming tired.

The healing techniques presented in this book require discipline but eventually, we will be able to take our attention to any point in the universe for healing and support - whether we connect with an angel, a guide, a zodiac sign or a specific Ascended Master such as Mother Mary, Lakshmi or Jesus. This will be of immense value when we move onto magickal rituals for healing and intuition in the last chapter. Stay with this for at least two weeks, strengthening your channel, before moving onto the next.

Exercise 3: Chakra Balancing Technique

Now that we have some practice running energy through the body and activating our palm Chakras, the next step is to work with this energy while we scan and balance the Chakras. We can choose to work with all of them, spending a few minutes on each energy center, or instead focus our efforts on the one that needs it most, based on the creative Chakra healing questionnaires in the previous chapter. Or just trust your intuition to guide you, scanning your Chakras with your mind's eye for clues on their health.

1) Ground Yourself. With your feet planted firmly on the ground, visualize an oak tree growing strong behind you. Its broad trunk supports your back perfectly. Next, you are going to visualize tree roots growing out of the bottom of your feet into the ground. They cut through layers of dirt, rock, and lava, anchoring you to Mother Earth. The Earth's nourishing energy flows up these roots, through your legs to your Root Chakra, at the base of the spine. Your Chakras spin and the energy comes to rest in your Heart.

2) Attune to Universal Light. Still firmly grounded, you are going to take your attention up through the atmosphere, past the stars to the highest source of light in the universe. Visualize a beam of light traveling down through towards your Crown Chakra. Your light body expands as it is touched by this loving energy, which flows down your core to your Heart Chakra. It activates your natural healing abilities. Earth energy and universal light to flow from your Heart, down your arms to the palms of your hands.

3) Ask for Permission. In school we were taught to ask for permission before carrying out a healing. The green light comes from our soul – ask quietly and listen for an answer in your heart. In most cases the response will be affirmative. We do sometimes get a "No" if the time is not right for healing, or if we are focusing on an end result that is not in alignment with the highest good of the person receiving the healing energies.

4) Protect Your Energy. Visualize a bubble of pink or green light around your Aura, creating a safe and loving environment for you to explore your feelings. This light protects you and facilitates the energy healing process.

Note: We can memorize the first four steps by using the term "Mind the GAPP" - an acronym from my student days at the School of Intuition & Healing - alluding to the grounding, attuning, permission, and protection steps.

5) Feel the Energy in Your Palms Once again, we bring our palms together and visualize a sphere of light between them, staying with this visual until the energy starts to build, before we move onto balancing the individual Chakras.

6) Scan Your Chakras. There are different ways to scan our energy centers. We can take our attention to each of the Chakras, tuning in and asking it to give us a color, a feeling or a sensation. Trust what comes to you, for example, if you see brown flecks in the Solar Plexus Chakra which is usually yellow, would that indicate the need for healing? Don't judge the visual or respond to it emotionally. Whatever we find is merely an intuitive message, a symbol that we can interpret as part of the healing process.

Another option could be to scan your Chakras with your left, receiving hand. Start by taking a few deep breaths and hold your left hand close to your Crown Chakra, palm facing inwards. The Chakra in your left hand connects with the Crown, sensing its energy. You may feel tingly sensations, temperature changes and you may even see colors flash through your mind's eye. If you feel the Crown needs healing, use your right hand to fill it with light. When you are done, move onto the Brow with your left hand.

We can go through each of the Chakras this way – personally, I find it easiest to scan all of my Chakras with my left hand before balancing them with my right hand. This can help us distinguish between a vibrant Chakra and one that needs more attention, as we move from one to the next. Start by holding your left hand between your Brow and Crown, and then slowly bring it down the front of your body.

7) Go Deeper. If a specific Chakra needs extra care, bring your left palm back to that position and close your eyes. See yourself standing in that Chakra – a miniature version of yourself. Use your imagination and your intuition to visualize it. You might see it as a colorful tunnel through which you walk, sensing its energy. Give yourself a few moments to get an unbiased view of that Chakra and then fill it with light, intending for that light to clear any memories, worries, fear or outdated beliefs that could be held there. That light flows through the Chakra to the area of life that it governs, such as love through the Heart or personal power through the Solar Plexus. Thank the light for the healing, asking that it fill you with love.

8) Close and Shield Your Energy. Always end the healing process by disconnecting from the source of light. This protects your energy and makes it possible for you to go about your life without any psychic windows being left open. To do this, take your attention up to that star and thank it for its healing light. Gently disconnect and follow the fading beam of light back to your Crown Chakra. Draw your Aura in around you and let your Chakras switch off one by one, no longer sensitive to the energy around you. Place a bubble of protective light around your body and open your eyes. Write down your impressions so that you do not forget them.

Healing Tip! The more we practice meditation and self-healing, the easier it becomes. If you are new to energy healing, it can also help to practice on someone else. Practicing will make it easier for you to trust your intuition and any impressions that surface. Go through the grounding, connecting and protecting steps before using your left hand to scan their energy. Have fun with it and do not be afraid to speak up! The quirkiest impressions are usually on the mark. As you will see in the next chapter, there are seven psychic abilities so don't worry if you do not see anything during a session. Impressions can come as feelings, physical sensations, temperature changes or thoughts that come and go in an instant.

My Diary of a Psychic Healer blog is also a great resource for student Healers, as I invested a great deal of time documenting my experiences with both energy healing and intuition. The following is an excerpt from an article called My Personal Experience with Chakra Work – a homework assignment for healing school.

Diary of a Psychic Healer, 12th March 2011

"Working with the Chakras is exciting, kind of like exploring uncharted territory. It took me a few weeks to get to the point where I was comfortable with finding them on the body. That was an exciting process that I will go on to describe below. Since then I have been pleasantly surprised during most of my healing sessions. Over the course of my studies I have been able to sense the Chakras in three different ways, the first being mental images, the second temperature changes, and the third physical sensations. For this assignment, I decided to separate the 2nd and 3rd as they served a different purpose.

When I started learning energy healing I was a little bit lost as to where the Chakras were placed. I asked Spirit to give me a sign when my hand was in the right spot, and it gave me temperature changes. My hands would usually feel heat throughout the session, and I started to notice that this sensation turned to cold when my hand was over the areas I came to identify as the Chakras. This went on for a few weeks until I became a little bit more confident about the location of the Chakras in the physical body. On some occasions I felt cold when I wasn't working on the Chakras, and took it to mean that I should stay there for a while. Overall temperature really helped me find my way during healing sessions.

Next I began feeling prickly sensations when there was a lot of energy coming through. This prickly sensation evolved into a flow of energy that my imagination saw as white light. This is when my experience with the Chakras started to involve clairvoyance, in the form of mental pictures and visions. At first I saw this as pure white light flowing through the Chakras, and I would count beats in my head until it was time to move on. One day, this white light turned to gold after 10 beats, and I took it to mean that my time there was up. This method helped me establish a rhythm to the healing sessions, especially when I am under time constraints during a healing session.

When I had gotten used to the pace of a 15-20 minute session, I stopped looking for that gold light and started seeing colors instead.

For example, on one occasion I noticed that my client's Solar Plexus was bright yellow with a twisted black cord going through it. It was striking because the colors were very defined and the contrast between the yellow Chakra and the black cord were impossible to miss. During the next session, I noticed that her Heart Chakra had a lot of orange in it. It didn't feel angry, but I did get the impression of a very passionate attitude towards life. After the session she mentioned that she was tired because she felt like she needed to pour her heart into her work and her relationships, and was frustrated that she didn't get the same in return. This helped me understand the link between our daily life and our subtle energy body.

Finally, on a few occasions I have felt tightness, electricity or even discomfort in my own Chakras and /or in my body. It doesn't happen very often, when it does it's usually at the beginning when I'm just tuning into the person's energy. This will let me know what to focus on during the session, and where to direct my attention if I have time left over. On one occasion I felt a constriction in my throat when I was going to ground the client. I went back to that area for another minute before proceeding to ground her. This has only happened a handful of times; the reading tool I use most often is color and shapes.

My last point regarding the Chakras has to do with tracking the progress the Healee makes. It's helpful to see colors and shapes, especially if you take notes on how the Chakras evolve over a series of sessions. One of my clients started the sessions with a very dim Crown Chakra; at the third session it was funnel shaped and a very light blue. By the last session it had grown into a clear cylinder, and when I discussed this with her she was very happy to learn that her Crown had opened up, as that would eventually strengthen her connection with God, the universe and with her angels too. It was pretty cool because you can talk about it in very concrete ways that both the Healer and the Healee understand and remember."

Sensitivity builds with time so do not worry if your impressions are much fainter to begin with. In Chapter 6 we will introduce exercises to strengthen your intuition. In the meantime, know that all the meditations and exercises in this book lay the foundations for your intuition to develop.

Exercise 4: Healing Across Time and Space

In my student days, one of the most mind-blowing classes was distant healing. The theory was that we could send that same healing energy across time and space to heal a person at a different location. Even after months as a student Healer I couldn't quite wrap my mind around that idea – I thought it had to be more diluted than giving healing in person. My teachers laughed when I said as much and suggested that I get on with the exercise. They had lined us up across two sides of the room, sitting ten feet away from each other in pairs. We were guided through a similar meditation to the ones described above, only, this time, we would bring that earth and universal energy together in our Heart Chakras and then project it from the Heart, across the room to our classmate. We were also supposed to tune into their energy and get a sense for where they might need healing, directing the flow of energy in their bodies.

When the time came for me to receive healing, I was quite literally blown away by the rush of energy coming my way. It might have been stronger than the rush of energy I usually felt when I was receiving healing from a person who was standing in my Auric field with their hands just a few inches away from my body. I can't explain it, but distant healing sessions turned out to be as powerful as regular sessions.

In this chapter we will focus on a specific process for distant healing that ties in nicely with the magickal rituals in the final chapters. Before you begin you may want to find a stuffed animal or a crystal.

1) Intention. Begin by asking yourself what or who you would like to focus on. Is it another person that needs healing, or would you like to focus on a memory that came up during your Chakra explorations? We can also send healing to the future, i.e. calmness during a job interview.

2) Grounding. Use one of the techniques in Chapter One to ground your energy, whether it's visualizing tree roots, running energy through your legs or simply the intention to ground.

3) **Attune.** Take your attention up through the atmosphere to that pure source of light. Bring that light down to your Heart Chakra where it mixes with Earth energy and activates your Aura.

4) **Permission**. If we are healing someone else, we ask his or her soul or Higher Self for permission.

5) **Carry Out The Healing.** We do this by visualizing that energy flowing from our Heart Chakra, down our arms to the proxy that we have chosen. It might be a crystal, a stuffed animal or we could sit outdoors with our hands on the Earth, asking that it deliver the healing to the moment in time that we have in mind, and to the person receiving it. I like to use a small Quartz sphere as a proxy. Or, we can place our hands on our Chakras and use them as a proxy. The healing energy travels through time and space immediately; the proxy just holds our attention to keep it going.

6) **Disconnect** and close down when you are ready to end the session.

I would suggest using this technique to send healing to any issues that may have come up during your Chakra explorations, especially patterns that seem hard to break. In Chapter 7 you will learn to clear and program crystals with specific, healing purposes. We then take the crystal with us to receive the healing.

Parting Words for Student Healers

Channeling healing is remarkably easy. Learning to trust and maintain the flow of energy is another story. In order to be effective and happy Healers, we need to keep an eye on the following elements:

The quickest way to drain your energy as a Healer is to become invested in a particular outcome. Whether it's wanting to prove that healing works, wanting to relieve someone's headache or wanting to help a loved one heal from a difficult disease; the more attached we are to the outcome, the worse off we will be. This attachment takes away from the efficacy of the healing and it also tires us out.

Developing a daily practice of grounding, clearing and shielding our energy makes it possible for us to give healing to ourselves and others without overloading our "psychic" senses in the process. While it can be very helpful to read the Auras and the Chakras during a session, we don't need to read everyone else's energy 24/7. Learning to ground, clear and shield your energy switches off the sensors when they are not needed. Without this, taking public transport could be a nightmare.

Begin healing in small increments and slowly work your way up. The energy that comes through during a healing can give us a high, followed by a crash when we come off it. Learning to channel healing without going through those ups and downs was one of my biggest lessons as a student. Practice is the only thing that gives us the capability to channel energy steadily, without a subsequent crash.

The more we meditate the stronger our channel becomes. Please find a meditation that you like – no longer than 10 or 15 minutes – and meditate often to build your energy and your intuition. In school we practiced these techniques every day for two years before sitting for our Healing Accreditation and it never got boring. Healing another person is like looking at the story of their life, with unique visuals, and plot twists. Their spirit guides can also pop in to help us find our way as healers and channels of light. The tools in this book map out the beginning, please sign up for an energy healing class to learn more.

Nothing beats an in-person class, but if you cannot find a teacher, I will be offering online lessons every week where we will explore energy healing & intuition through meditations and live workshops. Visit Diary of a Psychic Healer.com for details, and look for the "Sign Up For Class" tab.

Chapter 6
Psychic Development For Beginners

Starting on the path of psychic development can be exciting if not overwhelming. With so many themes to explore, where do we begin? Intuitive healing, mediumship, psychic astrology, shamanism, intuition and other types of energy work quite literally open up a world of possibilities. Regardless of the modality chosen, a strong physical and energetic foundation can pave the way for your development. The human body is more than a temple for your Spirit; it's also a channel for healing and psychic insights. We develop strong, clear channels by adopting a daily meditation practice and embracing our unique gifts. But first, let's begin with an important question ...

Where Does Intuition Come From?

When the phone rings we usually want to know who is on the other side. The same is true for intuitive messages, but first, let's ask ourselves: what is intuition? The dictionary defines it as "a feeling that makes a person act a certain way without fully understanding why." Webster's Dictionary references "a natural ability or a power that makes it possible for us to know something without proof or evidence." A hunch, if you will. Both of these definitions resonate with me. The only thing I would add is that intuition comes to us as a series of extrasensory messages. I honestly believe we are being given answers all the time. Every now and then we get a heads up too. The more we listen to these messages, the easier it is for us to navigate our way through life. But where does this information come from?

Who sends the message? As far as I can tell, intuition has two main sources: our spirit guides and angels, and our soul.

a) The Angels

Angels are sent by God to keep order in the universe, each with his or her unique mission. They are not affiliated with one religion but the belief in angels is more common in Christianity, Judaism and Islam. There are also hierarchies of angels, each with their own responsibilities. The ones we interact with the most tend to be assigned to Earth and to humanity. Guardian angels look after individual humans, guiding, protecting and inspiring us – while the Archangels look after specific themes like childbirth, healing, love, creativity, courage, beauty, art or life path and soul missions. The Archangels are what you would call lieutenants in an army of angels, each with thousands under their command to help us out.

When I call on the angels, I find it easiest to reach out to my Guardian Angel as she is assigned to me, and to Archangel Michael, the angel of courage and protection, because Michael is also the boss of all the other angels. I simply ask Michael to send the angel that will help me with the problem at hand. Angels do not have a will of their own (but they do have a mind of their own, coming up with creative ways to help us when the time is right) and their divine mission is to assist humanity and the Earth, with the good of all in mind. They won't help us out if it will be at the expense of another, instead looking for a win-win situation. While there are fallen angels, we will instinctively know whether we can trust the angel that turns up by tuning into the feeling in our Heart Chakra. Michael can also help us to discern it.

We can also choose to reach out to an individual Archangel based on their theme. The Archangels are multifaceted and I am often surprised to see who turns up with a message about a particular request. Nevertheless, these are some of the areas that the Archangels are often associated with:

For Courage: Archangel Michael looks after the peacekeepers of the world, helping those who cannot defend themselves. We can support his mission by volunteering our services to humanitarian causes. We call on Michael for courage, strength, determination and protection.

For Healing: Archangel Raphael's mission revolves around health. We can pitch in by comforting the sick and by teaching others to ground and center their energy, hopefully bringing balance to the world. We can call on Raphael for healing, and ask him to guide health workers.

For Communication: Archangel Gabriel looks after artists, journalists, mothers and those who lack a voice in society. We can support his mission by speaking up for vulnerable adults, children and animals. He (or she) can also help us with self-expression, intuition and writing.

For Guidance: Archangel Uriel works behind the scenes, sending guidance on our life path. We can support Uriel's mission by mentoring others and coaching them through tough times. When we are in need of guidance ourselves, Uriel sends someone to help us find our way.

For Intuition: Archangel Haniel is a healer and she also enhances our intuition. She is often associated with the moon's phases and with Venus's healing powers, which are based on love.

For Beauty and Artistic Inspiration: Archangel Jophiel inspires artists of all kinds, helping them channel abstract energies into painting, sculptures, film and photography. He also helps beautify our thoughts.

For Love: The angel of unconditional love, Archangel Chamuel fills our heart, mind and body with love so that we can learn to give and receive. He teaches us to love ourselves, and others.

For Prayers: Archangel Sandalphon is the angel of prayer. He is said to listen to our thoughts and what is in our hearts, taking our requests up to the spirit world where they are processed.

The more we connect with the Archangels, the easier it becomes for us to work as a coordinated team. Whereas spirit guides tend to coach us from the sidelines, the angels step in to catch the ball and run with it when we need to score a touchdown and can't get to the end zone ourselves.

b) Spirit Guides

These wise souls are most often human beings that have led an earthly existence in the past, one where they excelled in a specific area. They coach us from the other side so that we can make the most of their knowledge, before coming back to Earth to continue developing other skill sets. So for example, we might have a guide who was a champion when it came to science, business and technology but not so great at personal relationships. Until they are ready to come back to work on their relationship skills, they coach us from the other side on all matters pertaining to science and technology. We often have a single guide with us through life to coach us on our major lessons, and temporary guides that come and go as we embrace new challenges and growth opportunities. For example, a Reiki practitioner may have a healing guide during her whole life, and a temporary parenting guide when her children are teenagers.

Spirit guides usually communicate intuitively, guiding us with coincidences and chance encounters. If we learn to connect with them in meditation we can make their jobs and our lives a lot easier. They can also give us clues on our life purpose and hidden talents. This is how I got into healing. Years ago I was enrolled in a creative writing class. We were tasked with writing a short story and one of my characters spontaneously healed a person after a car accident. I hadn't planned on including an accident, or the healing, the images flashed through my mind and I couldn't have been more surprised. Funny enough, the way I described the healing and the bruised Aura was remarkably similar to how I experience it now. I enjoyed writing it so much that I thought I would write a novel, and spent months researching miracles, healing and other psychic phenomena to make it as real as possible. I never did write that novel but the research continues!

Spirit guides tend to introduce themselves in funny ways so don't be surprised if the following happens:

- You ask to see your guides during a meditation and you see a pair of feet, a color floating in the air or even hat and a pair of glasses. Spirit guides reveal small clues, particularly in the beginning.

- Our guides tend to adopt a persona that resonates with our personal affinities. As Denise Lynn points out in her book - Past Lives, Present Miracles - the time periods we feel drawn to can often be a reflection of our past lives and what they have to offer. If you sense your guide as a South American shaman, for example, studying that religion or practice will enhance your development.

- When we begin to recognize their energy, they may change shapes to highlight different aspects that need to be addressed. For example, I have a spirit guide who would always turn up in a wizard robe and a pointy hat. Initially, I thought he had to be a figment of my imagination until my classmates began seeing him too. After I had been working with him for years, he began to show himself as a young boy, enthusiastic about his magickal explorations and totally fearless (as kids can be). The message was for me to reconnect with that childlike wonder and adventure.

c) Your Higher Self

There is a part of us that forgets who we are the moment we are born, all of our soul memories and unique skills are buried in the unconscious or perhaps on a distant star, in the Akashic Records. The part that doesn't forget is your Higher Self – or your spiritual self, your soul. We can access this wisdom through our unconscious and our intuition. Our Higher Self understands the role we chose in this life, why we chose it, and where it can take us in this life and future lives. When you are at a loss for words or struggling to find your path, the most accurate GPS instructions come from your Higher Self.

d) Messages from the Ego (not our Intuition)

We also receive messages that are fabricated by our fears, and part of the challenge early on is learning to differentiate between the two. If the message is timely, useful and empowering—even in tough situations—know that it comes from the light. If it scares us or plays to our fears, it is likely from the ego. Our angels and guides will always help us find a way to improve on a difficult situation, or to tolerate it.

e) The Client's Energy and Guides

If we are using our intuition to read another person's energy, whether it is during an energy healing session or a psychic reading, the source will be twofold. Some psychic impressions will come directly from their being, for example, colors that we may see in the Aura and the Chakras. Our healing guides and their angels and guides will most likely be on hand too, pointing out elements that need to be seen.

We can begin to sense our angels and spirit guides with this meditation:

- Ground yourself by visualizing concrete boots on your feet.
- Surround yourself with violet light for protection, as your Aura grows stronger and larger. Ask your angel or guide to make their presence known – you may sense a color or a vibration.
- Check with your Heart; if you don't get a good feeling simply tell them to leave. We control who has access to our energy field.
- When you are done with this meditation, bring your Aura back to regular size and protect yourself with a bubble of violet light.
- Make a note of any feelings or impressions.

Activating Your Energy Field

The human energy field is like a sponge. Once it has been attuned to spiritual energy, it soaks up everything we come into contact with. This can help us during energy healings and readings, though it is also important to clear our energy and close down at the end. Otherwise we may go about our daily lives feeling psychic debris on the morning commute, taking on a colleague's cold symptoms or even owning a loved one's distress. As healers and intuitives, we want to be there for the world without feeling it so intensely. This is a phenomenon that empaths will recognize. This is where the most basic principles of energy management come into play. By learning to ground, clear and protect our energy, we are able to access our intuition comfortably. These concepts are important in energy healing but even more so when we activate our intuitive reading skills. Otherwise we can become psychic dustbins.

In addition to grounding, clearing and protecting our energy as we have done, we will also learn to expand our Aura so we can sense the spiritual world, and to close down when we are done. This enables us to receive clear and specific messages when we are working. We always close down at the end to keep from being bombarded by the psychic and energetic interference around us. If you would like to stay open to see how it feels, prepare to feel tired, overwhelmed and a bit grumpy too. If this happens, a good energy clearing and grounding will put an end to it. Always shield yourself when you are done. The following steps will teach you to open up and close down safely. I do this before every reading whether it is tarot, angels or astrology. Soon these steps become second nature.

An Opening Meditation

1) Clear your Space. Visualize the brightest of white lights as it flows in through the ceiling and washes through the room, clearing imperfections and engulfing you in a cocoon of the purest healing vibrations.

2) Ground Yourself. See and feel as two beams of light shoot down through the ground from the soles of your feet to the center of the Earth. Those beams of light connect with the Heart of Mother Nature.

3) Activate Your Chakras. That light travels up through the Earth to your Root Chakra at the base of the spine, which turns bright red. The light then activates each of your Chakras, illuminating their orange, yellow, green, blue and violet energies, and continues up through your head to the sky.

4) Expand Your Aura. Bring your attention back to the room, visualizing these endless beams of light above and below you. Bring your attention to your Aura, now full of light, and activate every last layer.

There are many variations on this basic opening meditation. Sometimes we visualize a bubble of light around our bodies and call on our angels or guides from the outset. Other times we might picture ourselves as a massive tree and follow the roots up through the trunk to the uppermost leaf. The process of grounding ourselves deep in the Earth and then reaching up to the sky activates our energy.

A Closing Meditation

1) Disconnect from the Light. Take your attention back up to that source of light, thank it for activating your energy and bring your attention back to Earth as those beams of light fade away, above and below.

2) Zip Up Your Chakras. We are going to visualize a zipper down our body, from top to bottom. We zip down to close down our energy, observing as each of our Chakras switch to off position, one by one.

3) Shield Your Energy. Bring your Aura back to a comfortable size, ideally an arms length all around. Replace the beams of light at your feet with tree roots for grounding, and shield yourself with light.

The more often we practice these meditations, the more effective they become. We can guide ourselves through a daily meditation by calling on our guardian angel, opening up to chat, and closing down again.

The Seven Psychic Abilities

Adopting a daily meditative practice makes it easier for us to access our intuition. These messages are processed by the Chakras, the Aura and the body before we notice them. Meditation strengthens the channel through which these insights flow, enhancing our ability to receive clear messages. There are seven abilities though only a few are well-known – be open to receiving messages in a variety of ways:

1) Psychic Visions: This is typically known as clairvoyance. This is when our Third Eye pops open and we see an image in our mind's eye, whether it's a color, a shape, a person, a symbol, a tarot card or even an animated cartoon. Every now and then you may sit in a person's Aura and see images around you but for most people, clairvoyance happens in the mind's eye. Seeing these images is one thing and learning to interpret them is another. When we are reading for another, it helps to describe the visual before we try to offer an interpretation. There have been plenty of times when the sitter recognized an image that made no sense to me. Do not feel pressure to know all of the answers; that is not how it usually works.

As an example, a few years ago my classmates and I were giving readings at a psychic fair. A couple came in and mentioned that their son had passed away a few years earlier. During the clairvoyant meditation I kept getting an image of the mother writing a book, others reading it and seeing how they would be healed by her words. Only a parent who had been through the same loss could counsel others in such a heartbreaking situation. I also saw an image of a butterfly with children playing nearby. This made no sense to me. When I went on to give her the reading she told me that she had begun to write the book but stopped, wondering if it was worth the effort. The cover that she had in mind was just that, a butterfly in a park. The message was clear; Spirit wanted her to know that her book served a purpose.

2) Psychic Sounds: Also known as clairaudience, this is when we hear words, sounds or music. In my experience hearing voices is not common. Instead we receive clairaudient messages in the form of thoughts and mistake them for our own, unaware that our angels and guides send those thoughts. For example, back in my corporate days a thought would pop into my mind, telling me to look into a specific project (usually at the bottom of my priority list). Hours later my boss would come around asking me about that project, and I soon learned to recognize those messages as intuitive prompts from my Higher Self or my guides. After a few weeks I decided to enlist my guardian angel as a project manager, asking her to remind me when anything big was looming on the horizon. The more attention I paid to her messages, the more impressed my line manager became. A quick word was all I needed to stay on track.

3) Tactile Sensations: This is one of my favorites when it comes to angels. We may feel a feather brush against our cheek when we ask them for help, as a sign that they are near. As Healers, we may also feel a client's physical discomfort and that impression guides the healing session. If we are receiving this in a healing capacity, we thank our guides for the information and release the sensations by clearing ourselves with a shower of white light. Otherwise our bodies and Aura may hold onto to the discomfort.

4) Psychic Smell: This is when we detect a fragrance that is not really there. In my experience, psychic smell is most common when a loved one has passed away and is trying to contact us. We may get a whiff of their perfume, of tobacco if they smoked, and even unpleasant odors if there was a connection.

5) Psychic Taste: Similar to the above, we taste something, maybe apple pie or vinegar as a signal. Ask yourself what that taste means and if it reminds you of anything. These messages can be subtle, especially if they are from loved ones. Our family and friends are less experienced with communication than angels or guides, and they often send fragrances and flavors to get our attention. If we suspect that a particular scent or taste is from a loved one, it can help to ask a family member about the significance.

6) You Just Know: This is what most of us identify as intuition – we just know that something is right or wrong for us but we can't offer a rational explanation. These insights are usually processed from our environment by our Aura, or they come from above through the Crown Chakra and settle in our Heart.

7) Empathy: This may be one of the most useful psychic abilities but also the least comfortable. Empaths can sense what another person is thinking or feeling. While these insights can be very helpful in healing sessions, they can be overwhelming in daily life and learning to ground, clear and protect yourself is vital. When we receive such strong impressions we are usually meant to act on it – tuning into the feeling and asking our angels and spirit guides how to help the other person heal and release it. We often need to release the sensation ourselves, with a shower of light, or risk holding onto those feelings.

If empathy pains are a problem, protect your energy by grounding and clearing yourself on the spot before shielding the Root (physical) and Sacral (emotional) Chakras with a gold disc, front and back. Place your hand over your Sacral Chakra and tell your energy to send the impression into the ground. If we do not protect our energy consciously, the physical body may gain weight to add a protective layer.

Our Intuitive Processing Unit

We receive most psychic insights through the Chakras and the Aura. The upper 'metaphysical' Chakras, allow us to access clairaudience through the Throat, clairvoyance through the Third Eye and that sense of knowing through the Crown. They show us the big picture, indicating why obstacles arise and how to navigate our way through life. This intuitive guidance helps us find and follow our bliss, though we also need solid grounding and strong Root and Sacral Chakras to manifest those visions as a physical reality. The lower Chakras also act as sensors for physical impressions, empathy and what we call *gut feelings*.

We can discover aspects of our personality that need healing by exploring the seven Chakras and their themes, or by healing the Root Chakra at the base of the spine and working our way up. Each of the Chakras relates to a psychic ability and by working our way through all of them, we unlock our gifts.

The following is a simple exercise to expand your Chakras.

- Ground yourself by visualizing roots and shield yourself with light.
- Bring your attention to your Root Chakra; see it spinning brightly.
- Use your intention to expand this Chakra's diameter and length.
- Stay with this for a minute and bring it back to a comfortable size.
- Hold your hands over your Root Chakra and fill it with gold light. Intend for any debris to fall through your roots, into the ground.
- When the healing is done, ground and protect yourself.

We can repeat this process with each of the Chakras, working our way up from Root to Crown. Some of our Chakras may be easier to respond than others – don't worry; these may just take a little extra work.

Take Care of Your Physical Body

A well-rested and nourished body will make for a clearer channel, whether we are channeling healing or accessing our intuition. Take care of yourself by getting enough sleep, exercising, eating healthy foods and drinking plenty of water. Coffee, alcohol and other substances may turn the dial down on your intuition, although everyone responds differently. Keep a self-care diary to find out what works for you. There are those who recommend vegan, vegetarian, gluten free or dairy free diets to enhance healing and intuition. Personally, I have never ascribed to any of these diets and my intuition still works well. I also drink soda and coffee more often than I should. Recently I became a weekday vegetarian for environmental reasons and I cannot say that it has had any effect on my healing or intuitive skills. Everyone is different - if you would like to make changes to enhance your abilities, observe the results.

The one thing that does make a massive difference is meditation – the more we meditate the easier it becomes for us to see and feel our spirit guides. These don't have to be clairvoyant meditations. We can practice mindfulness, prayer, Tai Chi, yoga or even a whole host of creative meditations. To learn more about various fun and engaging meditation styles please read my OM Times Magazine article: 10 Creative Meditation Techniques (at omtimes.com) On the next page I have included an in-depth psychic meditation that will guide you through space clearing, grounding, activating each of your Chakras and meeting your guides. These are good to do once a week, in addition to the shorter, daily meditations in Appendix 1.

Please visit my Regina Chouza Youtube Channel for self-healing and clairvoyant meditations - or catch one of my monthly webinars, which are always announced in the weekly email newsletter. If you have yet to subscribe, please visit DiaryofaPsychicHealer.com and enter your details.

The Psychic Flowerbed Meditation

In this meditation we ground our energy, activate each of our Chakras and then embark on a journey to meet our angels and our guides. While I have uploaded it to my YouTube channel, I would also suggest recording yourself and playing it back. Your energy responds best to your own voice.

1) Space Clearing:

- Find a quiet place to sit, one where you will not be disturbed. Have a look around the room before closing your eyes: notice the décor, the furniture and the color pattern. Take a couple deep breaths to calm your mind and release your day. Breathing in love and peace, breathing out stress and tension.

- Bring your attention to the soles of your feet and let them relax. Work your way up through your ankles, calves and thighs letting any tension fall through the floor to the center of the Earth. Breathe into your stomach and release any tension from your abdomen and chest. Let your attention go up through your shoulders and neck to the top of your head, relaxing as you go. Take another deep, relaxing breath.

- With your eyes still closed, picture the room in your mind's eye. What color are the walls? Are there curtains on the windows, hardwood floors, rugs or carpets? Let these images flash before your eyes for a moment, and then watch as they are washed away by the brightest of lights. This light sweeps around the room. This light clears, heals and releases the energy as it goes. See and feel yourself bathed in light.

- Only the highest vibrations can coexist with this light, letting your angels and spirit guides in and nothing else. Continue to breathe in light as the ceiling lifts off, carried by the strength of that light. The physical space around you, and your body, are flooded with white light that continues to pour in from on high.

2) Connect With Mother Nature

- Bring your attention back to the soles of your feet, where your foot Chakras connect you with Mother Earth. See and feel these energy centers as they open up ever so slightly. You are going to ground yourself by creating a set of grounding cords, and having them go down to the center of the Earth.

- Your imagination brings these cords to life, as you see them cut through layers of dirt, rock and lava before reaching a beautiful cave at the center of the Earth. There, we find a huge crystal formation, right at the heart of the Earth. Let your intuition give it a color, indicating the healing that you need right now.

- Your grounding cords draw on the crystal's energy. It travels up the cords, to your feet where it brings tingles and warmth to your body. The energy flows up your legs to your Root Chakra.

- That energy releases any doubt or fear from your body and your psyche, firmly anchoring you in a place of love. Release any tension into the ground through your legs, for cleansing and renewal.

3) Activate The Lower Manifesting Chakras

You will now activate your Chakras, unlocking their intuitive gifts:

- Visualize the **Root Chakra** spinning a deep red, full of life and vitality as it energizes your body. This makes it possible for you to get a tangible sense of your surroundings through physical Aura layer.

- Next, bring your attention to **Sacral Chakra** in the lower abdomen, where we feel emotions, creativity and appetite for life. See and feel as it is filled with bright orange light, activating your sense of empathy.

- Bring your attention to your **Solar Plexus**, bright yellow and full of sunlight. Know that it is safe for you to shine your light in the world and your life. You grow in confidence and personal power.

4) Enter The Heart's Intuitive Garden

- Now bring your attention to **the Heart Chakra,** where we receive the clearest guidance. Step into your Heart Chakra where you see a beautiful garden, blooming with love. Sit on the warm earth and visualize a grounding cord dropping from your Heart, through your Root to the crystal in the Earth.

- Still firmly grounded, turn your attention to the sky where you find the Sun's warmth and the Moon's intuition. Connect with these luminaries and bring their light through the atmosphere, to your garden where the light reaches your body.

- Bring that light down through your Crown, Brow and Throat Chakras. Ask that it release any memories, beliefs, and any ideas about who you are that no longer serve a purpose in your life.

- Now that you are firmly grounded and connected to the energy of Mother Earth and the sky, turn your attention to your garden. Look for weeds or dead flowers and remove them. In their place, you can plant new flowers, letting your imagination bring the colors to life. The colors in the garden represent the different psychic abilities that are available to us: red for physical sensations, orange for empathy, yellow to help us feels the vibes in our surroundings, sky blue for clairaudience, indigo blue for clairvoyance and violet or white for just knowing.

- We receive intuitive guidance in many ways; the colors that stand out merely clue you into your intuitive strengths. We can plant seeds for new flowers to grow and new abilities to develop. For now we will observe with compassion, showering the flowers with love and light. When you are ready, move onto the next step.

5) Call On Your Angels and Guides

- Find a place to sit and feel the energy around you, basking in the light. You are going to call one of your Spirit Guides or Angels. Don't be surprised if they present themselves as a bird or squirrel.

- Take a moment to feel your guide's energy and to get to know them: colors, vibes, scents, sounds, etc.

- Tell your angel or guide what is in your heart and on your mind – observe any feelings, thoughts, or sensations. The more often you come here; the stronger those intuitive messages will become.

4) Closing Down

- Visualize yourself in the garden and looking up at the sky, thank Father Sun and Mother Moon for their love, support and guidance. Disconnect from their lovely energy, knowing full well that they are always there for you and let your Crown Chakra close down gently. Your Brow and Throat Chakras follow suit.

- We are going to close and protect our Heart Chakra by visualizing a beautiful fence around the garden, and closing the gate behind us as we leave. Bring your attention back to your body on the chair. Draw your Solar Plexus Chakra in closer to your body, protecting it with a gold plate at the front and back.

- Follow suit with the Sacral Chakra, before bringing your attention to the Root. Draw in your Root Chakra just a little bit, so that it's still bringing in warm earth energy. Protect it with white light. Visualize your grounding roots, and place a bubble of protective light around your body.

When you are ready, open your eyes, stretch and have a sip of water. Give yourself some time to come around before getting up.

A Few Words For Psychic Students

Developing our intuition can be fun but there will inevitably be times when we frighten ourselves with something that we see, or that a fellow explorer sees in us. It is important to mention that we can very easily tune into another person's fears, or even project our own, without realizing that it is, in fact, an irrational fear within, and not an external threat that we have witnessed. This is one of the reasons why we began with grounding, clearing and protecting our energy – as well as healing – before moving on.

If we clear and shield our surroundings before beginning a reading, as we did in this Psychic Flowerbed Meditation, we create a safe space where we will not be disturbed by external energies. And of course, we can also heal and release these fears with journaling, healing, meditation and tarot contemplation. This will help ensure the clarity and purity of the messages we receive while preparing us for the next stage of the journey, which is working with magickal rituals and focused intentions to create a better future. If we haven't faced our hidden fears we are likely to keep manifesting them around us, as well.

If you ever feel like you have contacted a "guide" that isn't from a place of goodness, call on Archangel Michael and have him remove this energy from your presence. Shielding us is part of Michael's mission and he is always ready and willing to step in, clearing and shielding our space. I always have him on guard. The angels can be in many places at once; they are not limited by our three-dimensional reality.

Warning! Please carry out these meditations only when you are completely sober. Alcohol and other substances can diminish our ability to ground, clear and shield our personal space, and the room where we meditate. This can make it possible for us to bring in energies that we don't want to connect with. As long as we follow the grounding, clearing and shielding techniques in this book, and call on Michael before psychic meditations, we have nothing to fear. We can also ask our guardian angel to protect us..

Chapter 7
Crystal Magick For Healing

Congratulations! We have finally arrived at the final chapters of this book. If you have been practicing the meditations and the creative healing techniques, then you will be ready to work your magick. I find it helpful to begin with self-healing before practicing magick because our personality traits often determine whether our endeavors are successful. Even if we were to manifest an opportunity, we need fire in our nature to pursue the opening, clarity to find our way through it and grounding to be practical.

I have been practicing healing for years but magick is still relatively new to me. If there is one thing I have learned, magick and energy healing are not that different. Both involve directing energy for a specific purpose. With healing, the focus is on restoring balance to the mind, body and spirit. Magick can accomplish this too, whether we use crystals, candles or words to quantify our intent. So for example, we can program a crystal with an external goal, such as manifesting a book deal, finding a new job or renting a property. But I find it much more interesting to work magick on ourselves, transforming our energy so that we can become the person we are truly meant to be. We can even work with our astrology charts to facilitate the process, balancing out our energy with vibrational healing. Magick and self-healing can help us find that balance, whether we need more fire to give us ambition or more earth to ground our energy a bit.

In this chapter we will leverage the energy healing tools discussed so far, giving them a magickal slant. Rather than channel healing and direct it at the physical body, we will learn to charge crystals with specific purposes, whether it is for healing or to manifest an opportunity. But first, let's define magick:

- Brandy Williams, author of *Practical Magick for Beginners,* defines magick as "the power of choice."
- The controversial turn of the century magician, Aleister Crowley, defined magick as: "the science and art of causing change, on a material as well as a spiritual level, to occur in conformity with will."

For me, a magickal practice has three purposes. First, we create a sacred space for prayer, meditation and connection with the divine, whether you believe in God, Jesus, Jehovah or another spiritual being. Second, we ask our angels, our spirit guides and that divine figure to help us find our path. This guidance comes to us intuitively though we can also turn to tarot or runes for guidance. Lastly, we channel earth and universal energies with the intent to effect a change in the world, or in ourselves. From a karmic point of view, it is important to ask that this energy be channeled for the good of all, making it a win-win situation. When we work with the endless abundance in the universe, these solutions come naturally.

The rituals in this book are basic, laying the groundwork for more advanced rituals in the future. We will include the following elements in our rituals – which focus largely on crystal magick for self-healing.

1) Casting a Protective Circle: Similar to all of the space clearing visualizations so far, we are going to create a safe space to connect with the angels, archangels and spirit guides. We can use Amethysts or regular stones to draw a circle on the ground or merely visualize a circle of light, as we have done so far.

2) The Four Elements: We will begin to explore the elements of Fire, Water, Air and Earth. This book is meant to lay the groundwork for more advanced techniques in the future – as my next book is on astrological magick and how we can work with the planets, the zodiac and the elements for healing.

For now, let's begin by getting to know the four elements, their energy and their role in healing rituals:

- **FIRE** represents the drive to create, to grow and to expand spiritually. It can be linked to ambition, passions and leadership skills. We always light a candle to include Fire in our rituals. The Renaissance era magician, Cornelius Agrippa, tells us this is important because the angels are made of the same archetypal energy as fire; its use strengthens their presence around us.

- **EARTH** is about the material and physical world, the practical impulses that can take the dreams from the realm of fire and turn them into a reality. We use crystals, rock or salt to include Earth.

- **AIR** is representative of the mind, communication, and strategic thinking. It adds an element of logic to our plans. As a writer, I like to use a pen to symbolize Air in rituals (it is mightier than the sword). In traditional magickal circles, a ceremonial knife is used instead, known as an *athame*.

- **WATER** is all about sensitivity, emotions, intuition and relationships. Whereas Air thinks its way through a scenario to arrive at an answer, Water's intuition can give an equally accurate answer. We can include this element by filling a small recipient with H20 – I prefer small silver cups or dishes.

The tools used in magickal rituals should be used exclusively for that purpose, to keep their vibes clear. I will cover magick in depth in my next book, on astrological magick for self-healing and manifesting. For now we will limit ourselves to studying the elements and how they relate to our lives. Think back to the meditation prompts for the Brow Chakra in Chapter 4, specifically the one where we began studying a tarot deck to familiarize ourselves with the cards in the four suits of the minor arcana. The more we connect with the cards and develop an intuitive understanding of the images, the easier it will be for us to ask our angels and guides for guidance when we need it. While receiving direct messages is what we aim for, drawing a few tarot cards is a great way to ask for confirmation and double check our findings.

This will be particularly useful in our magickal and healing work, as each of the elements also corresponds to a specific layer in the Aura. If you recall the material presented in Chapter 2, the physical Aura layer governs physical sensations, the emotional Aura layer registers our emotional interactions, the Mental Aura layer reflects thoughts and beliefs, while the spiritual Aura layer holds our soul's blueprint. As you may have guessed, Air is linked to the mental Aura layer, Water to the emotional Aura layer, Earth to the physical Aura layer and Fire to the spiritual Aura layer. We can use tarot cards to connect with the unconscious, as the images we are drawn to will mirror the energy that needs to be healed, released or merely recognized within ourselves. We can do this by shuffling the four suits of the Minor Arcana and seeing what comes up in a reading, or by laying the cards face up, and letting our intuition guide us towards a particular theme. If we are drawn to the suit of Cups (Water) we would use the session to heal the emotional Aura layer with the use of crystals, healing and meditation. In this way, we can begin to heal memories and wounds in the unconscious by working with the elements and with tarot cards.

This is the relationship between the Minor Arcana (Tarot), the elements and the Aura:

Minor Arcana	Elements	Aura Layer
Suit of Pentacles	Earth	Physical
Suit of Cups	Water	Emotional
Suit of Swords	Air	Mental
Suit of Wands	Fire	Spiritual

Analyzing each of the cards is beyond the scope of this book, but we can make plenty of progress just by following the tarot meditation prompts in Chapter 4. Our intuition connects with the symbolism and the archetypes in the cards to tell a story. Turn to the reading list in Appendix 3 for more.

3) Angels for Guidance: We also call on the main Archangels to help us create a sacred healing space, with Raphael at the East, Michael at the

South, Gabriel at the West and Uriel in the North. By now their energies should be familiar to us, especially if we have been calling on them in our daily lives. If we need help with a specific theme, we can also bring in another angel, such as Jophiel for artistic inspiration.

4) Crystal Magick: We are going to use these rituals to charge crystals for healing, choosing one for each of our Chakras. When this is done we can take them with us in a little pouch, or use them in self-healing meditations. The latter is quite easy; lie down and place each crystal on its Chakra while you meditate!

By now we have learned how to ground our energy, clear a space, channel healing, sense our Chakras for imbalances and outdated beliefs – as well as a few creative healing techniques. If there are issues that linger and we haven't quite been able to shake them, this is where crystal healing comes into play. The tools and techniques that we have been practicing so far make up 85% of a magick ritual. Before we start practicing crystal magick for healing, let's take a few steps back and discover the crystal kingdom.

Crystal Healing 101

One of my teachers, a brilliant crystal healer by the name of Claudia Lechuga (from ONE Todos Somos UNO, Mexico) tells us that when the universe was created, Gaia saw all of the light in the stars around her and wanted a bit of it for herself. That light was given to us in the form of crystals, especially the Quartz variety. In ancient times they were said to power civilizations like Atlantis thanks to their internal structure and the huge amount of energy that they can absorb and transmit. When it comes to energy healing and magick we are drawn to crystals because of their capacity to record the intent we program them with, and of course, because of the way in which they radiate healing light and love back to us.

That said, it is important to care for our crystals, giving them a bit of healing in return! New acquisitions need to be cleared before we use them, to be sure we don't bring any extraneous vibes into our homes:

Clearing Newbies. Crystals radiate healing energy though they are also quite sensitive, absorbing vibes from their surroundings. It is important to clear new crystals before we use them because all crystals have a past; even if it was purchased from a shop, dozens of people will have handled it. I learned to clear crystals by placing them on a bed of rock salt or brown rice for an hour or two, and letting that clear their energy. There are other ways to clear them - running them through water, or placing them in sun or moonlight. Some crystals can lose their shape or color in water or sunlight, so it is always a good idea to check before trying either of those. As far as I know, rice isn't harmful and salt only affects a handful of stones. Don't leave them "clearing" for too long, as that can diminish the stone's properties.

Charging Them. Whenever we clear a space we have to fill it with light, whether it's a crystal, a house or a Chakra. Hold your crystal in your dominant hand and visualize light coming down from the Heavens, through your Crown Chakra, through your arm and to the crystal. Ask that it work for your highest good and healing. Specific crystals can also be programmed for love, prosperity, healing, abundance, forgiveness, etc. We will cover this in the next section when we look at crystals for the seven Chakras.

Quick Cleanse. You might hold a crystal in your hands and meditate, or lie down and place a variety of crystals on your Chakras. It is good to clear them after each session by running them under the tap for a few seconds. This is especially important if you use crystals for healing, yourself or others, as they often absorb energy during healings. This quick cleanse prepares the crystal for the next healing session. I also like to channel healing and send it to the crystal, for its own good, as a thank you for the healing it gave.

If your crystals are out in the open they will need to be cleared more often than those tucked away. In my experience, crystals that need clearing tend to fall away, dropping off pendulums and even bracelets.

Connect with Your Crystals

Once your crystals have been cleared in salt and filled with light to program them for your highest good, we can introduce ourselves to the spirit of the crystal. You will soon notice that they have personalities and that we can connect with them for guidance or just to lift our spirits. We can use the opening meditation from Chapter 5, where we visualize beams of light grounding us (crystals respond well to light), only this time, we are going to work exclusively with the Earth, leaving the sky and stars for later.

A Brief Crystal Meditation:

- Visualize two beams of light shooting down from your foot Chakras into the Earth.
- You connect with a huge Quartz crystal at the center of the Earth - it is full of sparkling light.
- Bring that crystalline energy up through the Earth, into your feet, up your torso and all the way to the crown of your head where it spills over, cascading through your Aura to your feet.
- Your Heart overflows with light – it flows down your arms to your palm Chakras.
- Hold the crystal in your hands and connect with it – pure light with pure light. Feel its energy and look inside it with your intuition. What do you see?

Finish by grounding yourself and thanking the crystal for choosing you. We can connect with all of our crystals this way so long as we have already cleared them to begin with, releasing the previous owner's energy. The goal is to reset the crystal to "factory conditions" and then begin to connect with its light.

Crystals for Chakra Healing

We can choose crystals based on their healing qualities, or just choose the ones we are drawn to based on their colors and the glimmer we receive intuitively. *The Crystal Movie* by Spirit Science has wonderful tips on how to choose crystals and use them in our daily lives (available on YouTube). For the purpose of this book, we will focus on healing the Chakras with crystal therapy. Below you will find a brief crystal guide, but this list is by no means exhaustive. Certain crystals work on several Chakras; Clear Quartz and Amethyst can be used on all of them, but I prefer to use Amethyst for general healing, as its energy is quite gentle. If you walk into a shop and are drawn to a crystal that is not on this list, look up its healing properties. You never know, it may be suited for an issue that needs attention at the time.

Root Chakra: Red Jasper, Black Tourmaline, Obsidian

The Root Chakra is our connection with Mother Earth. It also defines our energy levels and how safe we feel in the world. We can work with Red Jasper to ground out agitation while activating this red Chakra, infusing it with the planet Mars' drive, ambition and confidence. If feelings of safety are an issue, especially relating to any childhood problems (the Root develops by age 7), we can use Obsidian to transform fears and negativity, releasing them from our energy. Finally, Black Tourmaline grounds us.

Sacral Chakra: Carnelian, Bloodstone

The Sacral Chakra is about passion, creativity and appetite for life. It is also the Chakra through which we manifest dreams held in the Heart and Brow. Carnelian crystals can light the fire in our Sacral Chakra – think of the Sacral Chakra as a kitchen with lots of orders being sent out to diners. Carnelian gives us the firepower to keep creating (also increasing fertility!). Bloodstone will calm and energize relationships, removing any tension – hence the calming aspect – while filling it with passion and enthusiasm.

Solar Plexus Chakra: Citrine, Yellow Calcite, Yellow Jasper

The Solar Plexus holds our personality and our sense of self. Loving ourselves isn't possible unless we also love and embrace our human personality, quirks and all. Citrine is my favorite crystal for the Solar Plexus as it dispels any negativity, putting us in an "I can" frame of mind. It also empowers us through positivity and fosters abundance. Yellow Calcite is a recent discovery of mine: it also brings joy, dispels gloomy moods and helps us connect with Archangel Jophiel's bright and cheery energy. Finally, Yellow Jasper is a healing and soothing stone that works well with the stomach and how we digest ideas.

Heart Chakra: Malachite, Rose Quartz, Green Aventurine

The Heart is our gateway to unconditional love and abundance, and of course, it is also where we find our emotional heart – wounds and all. We can heal emotional hurts and memories by working with Malachite, a powerful crystal that can be used in polished form safely (raw Malachite can be toxic). Rose Quartz can be used if we need to learn to give and receive love without conditions, such as "if you do this, I will love your for it" or "if he loved me, he would do such and such a thing." Lie down and place a Rose Quartz crystal on your Heart Chakra, asking that the crystal work for your highest good. Open your Heart with an energy healing meditation and see how it feels to receive love from that crystal. We can also practice giving and receiving love by holding the crystal in our hands and circulating its energy through our arms, down the right and up the left. Once we have worked on healing ourselves with Malachite and Rose Quartz, we can open the doors to abundance by connecting with Green Aventurine, a stone that is associated with Jupiter, the planet of good fortune, expansion and lucky coincidences.

Throat Chakra: Lapis Lazuli, Fluorite, Turquoise

The Throat Chakra rules communication and our ability to take an honest stand in the world. Lapis Lazuli can help us clear emotional fog including any conditioning so that we can remember the truth of who we really are. A popular stone in Ancient Egypt, it was also associated with the multifaceted goddess Isis, who ruled the night sky and the stars as well as magick, healing and intuition. We can use Lapis to both see and hear clearly. Fluorite can help us digest complex metaphysical concepts, increasing our listening comprehension. We would benefit from working with Fluorite on all three of the metaphysical Chakras. Turquoise balances and heals the Throat Chakra because being a water stone, it establishes pathways for the Sacral Chakra's emotions to flow to the Throat, where they are naturally meant to be expressed.

Brow Chakra: Clear Quartz, Lapis Lazuli, Sodalite

The Third Eye rules our thinking skills, logic and intuition of the visual kind. We can work with Clear Quartz to remove limiting beliefs and thought patterns. Clear Quartz is also a fantastic stone for scrying, which is when we use water, mirrors or crystal spheres to awaken the Brow Chakra and receive images. Begin by meditating, relax your eyes and look into your Clear Quartz – soon you will start to see images flash across your mind's eye, aided by the crystal. Sodalite can help us merge logic with intuition for inspired and practical thinking. Lapis Lazuli helps us clear any emotional confusion so that we can see clearly.

Crown Chakra: Calcite, Clear Quartz, Sugilite, Amethyst

Just like the Root Chakra connects us with Mother Earth, the Crown is our connection to the non-physical world and all of its inhabitants, including the angels. White calcite is said to deepen our affinity with the angels, bringing us into their vibrational realm so that we can hear their messages clearly. Clear Quartz is fantastic because it can be charged with any purpose, and its clarity and purity bring us closer to that high vibrational healing light that we have been connecting with. Sugulite strengthens the bond we have with our spiritual self, and with divine love and wisdom, offsetting the traps of the human ego. Amethyst a wonderful stone for the Crown Chakra, boosting our intuition and our shielding.

These are not the only crystals that we can use to connect with the Chakras. If you are drawn to another please research its qualities – or acquire it, clear it and get to know its energy. Clear Quartz, Amethyst and Rose Quartz are good to start with, as we can cover all our bases with these.

Crystals for Aura Clearing

While all of the crystals come from the Earth (except for meteorites), their vibrations can resonate with different elements. Red coral for example, is imbued with the energy of Water as it comes from the ocean, and with Fire thanks to its bright red color. This is an excellent crystal to enhance our intuitive skills on both an empathy (Water) and spiritual inspiration

(Fire) level. We are going to use specific crystals in our healing rituals to clear, heal and balance our mental, emotional, physical and spiritual bodies (also referred to as the four Aura layers). The following are a few suggestions for Auric healing:

Physical Aura: Black Tourmaline, Amazonite, Sunstone, Quartz

Our physical Aura layer is closest to the body and as such, healers often sense "symptoms" in this layer before they manifest in the physical body as a cold, a sore throat, etc. Clearing and healing this Aura layer makes it possible for us to deflect colds, though we would never be able to prove it. We can also work on releasing childhood traumas and any memories that determine whether or not we feel safe in the world. These themes go hand in hand with grounding, which is why we can use Black Tourmaline (grounding) and Sunstone (deflecting negativity and bringing in light) to heal the physical Aura layer. Quartz is also a fantastic clearing stone, as we can program it with any intent and its laser-like focus does the job. Finally, Amazonite can be used to bring our physical body and our physical Aura into alignment again.

Emotional Aura: Moonstone, Coral, Chrysocolla

If we think about the element of water and everything it represents in a tarot deck, it becomes clear why we associate this with the emotional Aura layer. Moonstone can help us heal our emotions by connecting with the natural ebb and flow in the Earth's oceans and the moon's cycle. It slowly reveals what is hidden, making it easier for us to go into the unconscious gradually. It also heightens our intuition while making it easier for empaths to shield themselves with the moon's help. Coral helps us connect with the intuitive world of emotions and with the fiery element of passion, heating up what needs to be released so that it evaporates under some pressure. Both stones are wonderful for healers and empaths.

Mental Aura: Aquamarine, Moonstone, Citrine

The mental Aura layer is where we hold thought forms, beliefs and judgments made about ourselves in the past. So for example, if we lived through a rough experience the emotional charge will be in the emotional Aura layer but the belief we created about ourselves will be in the mental (don't worry if this is confusing, we can always use Clear Quartz to heal an incident on all layers). We can work with Aquamarine to relieve mental and emotional stress (thanks to the aqua). This soothing stone can also activate our clairvoyant abilities, stimulating our mental Aura and Brow Chakra. Finally, we can work with Citrine to infuse its sunny optimism in our mind and our energy field. Moonstone acts on both our emotional and mental Aura layers, calming the turbulent waters and clearing the sky (vision).

Spiritual Aura: Amethyst, Fire Agate

The spiritual Aura layer registers the truth of who we are on a soul level. When we think about Fire in relationship to the spiritual Aura layer, this spiritual fire embodies confidence, fearlessness and the drive to take action that comes when we embrace our purpose. As the outermost Auric layer, we can work with Fire Agate crystals to burn and release muddled energy on the three interior layers. Without that interference we will be better able to hear divine guidance and take definitive action. As the outermost layer, this is also where our shielding visualizations take effect; we can boost those with Amethyst.

Everything we have lived through is stored in the Aura, this is one of the reasons why healers and energy workers can pinpoint specific things that might have happened in the past. While that history will always be part of who we are, we can heal and release the emotional charge given to difficult experiences so that they no longer weight us down. There are crystals that can help us clear and heal the Aura across its many layers, and these will be helpful when we cannot pinpoint a specific layer, or if an issue ripples through several layers. Clear Quartz, Amethyst and Rose Quartz are wonderful all-purpose stones. The clear variety can be adapted to any healing purpose and we need only ask that it work for our highest good and healing. Amethyst takes any heavy, tense or stuck energies away and replaces them with love. Finally, we can work with Fluorite crystals, especially the rainbow variety, to repair tears in the Aura.

A Magickal Ritual for Healing

This is the ritual that I use myself, for guidance, healing and magick. We are just adding candles, a definite structure and a few extra tools to the healing meditations that we have carried out all along. This is not to minimize the value of magickal rituals, rather to highlight the fact that our intention creates the magick and the tools support it. There is however, a psychological benefit to following the structure of a ritual: your spiritual and energy body recognizes the process. This puts you, the magician in the right frame of mind. We can also choose certain colors for our altar, in line with the purpose of the ritual. When I am working with the Chakras I tend to choose candles and table cloths that match the Chakra: red for the Root, orange for the Sacral, yellow for the Solar Plexus, pink or green for the Heart, powder blue for the Throat, indigo for the Brow and violet or white for the Crown. If that is not possible, I use a white candle and do my best to keep an array of colorful paper napkins nearby. It is also quite easy to find a picture of a red, orange or yellow flower online and put that on your tablet or screen, etc.

Here are a few simple ritual steps:

1) Preparation:

Collect all of your materials so that you won't have to leave the ritual space once you begin. This includes candles, pens and journals for automatic writing, coloring books and crayons if you are using one of the creative healing techniques, crystals, tarot cards, and anything else you would like to use. A tidy room can help us keep our focus, so a bit of housekeeping can't hurt. Switch off your phone and any distractions.

2) Set Up Your Altar:

For me, the most important thing about an altar is that it be clear of distractions, holding only the tools and images for the ritual or the meditation. If I am just going to be meditating and journaling or doing a bit of energy healing, I will light a candle and use nothing else. If the goal is to work magick by charging a crystal with a specific purpose, I like to have all four elements on the table. Beyond that, you can use the same desk or nightstand every time, or adapt one wherever you are. It does help to have a set of tools that put us in the meditative ritual mode: a tablecloth, a candle, crystals and an image of the spiritual figure that you would like to reach out to. In my native Mexico, many rituals involve pictures of angels, Jesus or Mary as it is a predominantly Catholic country. When I lived in London my friendship circle was more diverse and we would see statues of Quan Yin the bodhisattva of compassion, or Lakshmi the goddess of prosperity. The key is to adapt the altar so that it resonates with the magician.

3) Light the Candle:

Once the altar is set up and you are sure you have everything you need, sit or stand in front of the altar and visualize a circle of light engulfing this sacred space. Ground yourself in Mother Nature and then light the candle. With this we solidify the intent to create a sacred space for us to connect with the angels, with our guides and channel their energy into our lives in a more focused manner. Stay with this image of light above, below and all around and feel the light within you growing stronger and stronger.

4) Call On The Archangels:

We are going to call on the four archangels and ask them to join us. They hold the space for us, keeping the energy high and pure. Raphael stands at the East, Michael at the South, Gabriel at the West and Uriel at the North. We are going to call on a fifth angel to assist with our magickal practice: Archangel Haniel, the angel of healing and intuition. She will oversee the proceedings so that all of our crystal healing and magick is in accordance with our highest good and not our whims or insecurities.

5) Meditate:

Take a few minutes to meditate on where you are in your life. How do you feel? Is there anywhere that you feel blocked? Close your eyes and scan your body and Aura from top to bottom, keeping an eye out for any colors, energies or even sensations that stand out. Visualize a stream of light flowing through you into the ground, as it clears and heals anything that you are now ready to leave behind. Sit with this for a few minutes and if you feel like journaling, ask your angels or your intuition to inspire your writing. This would be a good time to try the Automatic Writing technique.

6) Charge Your Crystal:

We charge our crystals using the same channeling techniques from Chapter 5, visualizing grounding roots going deep into the earth. The crystal at the center of the Earth is of the same color as the Chakra that we want to activate and heal – red for the Root Chakra, and pink or green for the Heart, etc. Draw that crystalline energy up through your grounding roots to your Heart Chakra and let it sit there, before taking your attention up through the atmosphere to the highest source of Light. Once both of those energies, earth and universal light, have come together in our Heart Chakras we are ready to begin.

Think of what you would like to achieve with this ritual. For example, is it a clear and healthy Solar Plexus, or healthy self-esteem and confidence? We are going to visualize the Chakra growing in size and power, spinning brightly and confidently as we draw that earth and universal energy into the crystal. Fill the crystal with healing light and ask that it activate and heal the Chakra in question. Stay with this for a few minutes, and visualize the benefits of a healthy Chakra system: how does it influence relationships, body image, energy levels, etc. See and feel yourself enjoying all of the wonderful things life has to offer.

If we are charging a crystal with the intent to purify the Aura, we visualize it being cleared and healed as any excess energy, imprints or beliefs are released into the ground for purification. This crystal is one that we would carry with us for one month, giving it a ritual booster every 10 days.

7) Close Down

In my experience, we are better able to focus our intent in rituals if we carry out one task at a time. In other words, I would perform seven separate rituals to charge the Chakra crystals, giving myself plenty of opportunities to connect with newly dedicated crystals and heal that Chakra before moving onto the next. When you feel that your crystal is fully charged, put it in your pocket or in a pouch. Thank your angels and healing guides for their assistance. Remember to close down by disconnecting from that source of light. Release the circle by walking in a counterclockwise direction along the perimeter. Thank the Archangels for their guidance and protection. Ground yourself by visualizing tree roots anchoring you to the ground, clear yourself with a shower of light and shield your energy with a bubble of violet light.

8) Record the Ritual

It is considered best practice to make a note of all of our magickal workings, so that we can come back to check our results later. While the crystal magick techniques in this book are very basic, continuing our studies and our practice will bring more elements into the mix. Keeping records makes it easier for us to know what works and what doesn't. For example, we might resonate with certain crystals and essential oils but not with others. Keeping records makes it easier for us to check our results and adapt our rituals. If you are working magick to shape your personality, for example to boost confidence, it can help to keep a diary and make a note of how you respond to different situations.

Magick Circle Tips!

- There will be times when we want to carry out a quick ritual and we don't have all of the props at our disposal. A burning candle is said to incorporate all four elements in the liquid wax (Water), the dry wax (Earth), the flame (Fire) and the air it consumes. If even that is not available, visualize that sacred space.

- You may choose to have ritual tools representing the elements on hand. Tools used in rituals should be reserved exclusively for rituals, and the first time we use them we consecrate them. This can be done with the "Distant Healing Method" from Chapter 5, where we channel Earth and Sky energy through our body to the distant healing prop in our hands – or in this case, to the ritual tool. So for example if you choose to use a pen to embody the element of Air, you would use your intention to dedicate it to Air.

- We can boost the power of the meditation by adding essential oils. Choose a scent that you are drawn to, or research their metaphysical properties. For example, there are oils for healing, mental clarity, grounding and abundance. Rub a few drops on your palms before charging the crystal talisman.

Timing for Rituals

We will not explore the timing of magickal rituals in too much detail, except to say that we can choose the day for a ritual based on the purpose we give it. All of the planets in our solar system have a day when their energy is stronger, and a theme that they can help us with. The planets that are associated with healing tend to be the moon (Monday) and Venus (Friday) so those are great days for Chakra healing. The moon is also linked with our emotions and our intuition, so Monday is a good day to perform healing rituals that will boost your intuition – perhaps with Moonstone or Amethyst. If we want to clear the mental Aura layer I would choose a fiery day as fire consumes air. Of the three planets associated with fire signs in the zodiac, the sun has the purest energy so I would choose Sunday. For emotional healing I might also choose Friday as Venus is associated with the Heart. Tuesday is a good day to work on increasing energy levels and vitality, and Saturday is good for grounding our energy. If you would like to learn more about practical magick and timing of events, I would suggest reading Brandy Williams fantastic book, *Practical Magick for Beginners*. Her book has been my favorite by far.

Chapter 8
Magickal Co-Creation

We can also work with crystals, candles and even drawings to manifest specific events in our lives, whether it's a new job, a new love, or a spectacular holiday. Whenever we do so, it is important to specify that it should come to pass "in line with the highest good" and that it "harm no one." We would not want to manifest the desired outcome but hurt ourselves or someone else in the process. It can also help to perform a divination before working any magick, asking our angels and spirit guides how that ritual would play out in real life. I would suggest using tarot cards or runes for this, though first we need to become fully proficient in reading them. Again, in my next book I will cover the astrological, magickal and manifesting tools that have worked well for me in the past. For now we will limit ourselves to manifesting abstract themes, such as love, money, health or career opportunities. We also focus on the energy or essence that we want to bring into our lives and how it will make us feel when we enjoy it, trusting the universe and our angels to deliver it in a package that is aligned with the highest good of everyone involved. This keeps us from setting our sights too low, or missing the mark, while creating something fabulous that will build with time as we continue to perform these rituals every month.

We can use the magickal ritual for healing outlined in Chapter 7, substituting these elements in the sixth step where we charged our crystals with a specific intent to heal and using the ritual for manifesting instead.

To summarize, our magickal rituals always include the following steps:

- **Prepare for the Ritual** by collecting your magickal tools and clearing any distractions, then set up your altar with all of the necessary elements.
- **Protect the Space** lighting a candle and visualizing a rush of white light around you. If you prefer to work with violet light that is alright too.
- **Call on the Archangels:** Raphael, Michael, Gabriel and Uriel to stand guard, Haniel to assist us by activating our intuition.
- **Meditate** on what you would like to co-create and consult your cards. If you do not see a favorable outcome in the cards, ask for more clarity.
- **Work Your Magick**, using the technique mentioned below for each purpose. You are going to focus on the feeling behind the experience or event, rather than on a specific outcome.
- **Release the magickal circle** in a counterclockwise direction, thanking your angels and guides for their help. End by grounding yourself and then clearing and shielding your energy with light.
- **Record the Ritual**, including the tools used and make a note of any psychic impressions.

The sense I get from the angels is that by working our magick, we partner up with them in carving out our path. These rituals combine focused intent and channeled energy during the session, followed up by action on our part to bring that alternate reality into being. Ideally we would listen to our intuition regarding the concrete steps that need to be taken, such as sending out resumes if we are job hunting, or approaching a specific building complex if we are looking for a new home or an apartment to rent.

Before we get to that point, however, we need to heal any blocks on an energetic level. For example, if we are trying to manifest love but our Heart (self-love), Solar Plexus (self-esteem) or Sacral Chakras (passion) are compromised, we first address this using the tools in Chapters 2-5 - identifying the relevant Chakra, exploring its issues and healing it. Chakra Healing is its own kind of magick. We can allow love, money, health and other kinds of abundance to enter our lives simply by healing the Chakras.

At this point, I would almost suggest that you meditate on what you would like to manifest in your life – whether it is love, money or laser sharp intuition - and reread this book from the beginning, focusing your efforts on the quality that you want to manifest and the Chakras that govern it. When that legwork is done, magickal rituals carried out to manifest an opportunity are more likely to give the desired result. We can also time our efforts with astrological transits to our natal chart, giving ourselves an extra boost. This goes beyond the scope of this Chakra Healing book - stay tuned for the next installment in 2017 or 2018.

With this in mind, the following rituals can be used to manifest love, health, and abundance. They operate on the assumption that we can only experience certain qualities on the physical plane if they are already part of our being on an energetic level – and that the timing is often beyond our control.

a) **Living Love.**

Tools: Rose Quartz, pencils or crayons, red or pink candles, paper.

We want to radiate love and let it permeate through every cell in our being. Sit in a quiet meditation and see and feel yourself filled with love and romance, using all of your senses and your creativity to bring it to life. You can do this by working with Rose Quartz crystals, which vibrate at the level of unconditional love, and holding the crystal against your Heart Chakra for 5-10 minutes. Let yourself feel that love, knowing that the crystals' loving vibration will grow with the strength of your self-love. Feel that love as it ripples through your Aura and out into space. Call on your guardian angel and ask that he amplify that love, creating a magnetic vibration will bring potential suitors to you, if they match your loving vibe.

If you are in a relationship already and want to dial up the romance, send out those loving vibes and see them filling your home, your work, every last sphere of your life. That feeling of wholeness, love and completion ripples over to your relationship, instead of looking to that relationship as the source of love.

Finally, we are going to create an image that represents the idea that we are love, that we live and breathe love, and that this abundance gives rise to romance, commitment and equal partnerships. We are going to draw this image with our colored pencils or crayons, using a process known as psychic art.

- Ground yourself by visualizing two beams of light going out of the soles of your feet, deep into the Earth. They plug into an orange, blue and violet crystal formation at the heart of the Earth.

- See and feel that crystal's energy as it travels up through the beams, through your body and out of the crown of your head. It continues through the atmosphere, to the highest source of light.

- Visualize those beams of light, above and below and ask Archangels Jophiel & Gabriel to appear. As the angels of art and self-expression, they fill you with inspiration while you draw.

- Take a red crayon or pencil and touch it down on the paper. On the of count three, you are going to take a deep breath, visualize a burst of romantic energy traveling down that beam of light from above, into your energy field, your Crown, to your Heart and down your arms. When that burst of romantic energy reaches the paper, your hand moves and you draw a red squiggle.

- Without lifting the pencil, close your eyes and ask your intuition for an image or a sensation that personifies a healthy, balanced, loving, committed, romantic and passionate relationship. Let it take shape in your mind and when it is at least thirty percent there, draw it on the paper. It doesn't matter how skilled we are as artists – only that we connect with that romantic energy.

- Keep asking for more images, drawing them one by one. Change colors when needed, and if you feel stuck, go back to that red pencil or crayon and put the point on the first squiggly shape. Continue drawing until you feel like you have captured the essence of the desired relationship.

- When you are done, write your full name and date of birth across the top of the image. Hold it between the palms of your hands and visualize that romantic energy flowing down from above, through your Heart and down your arms to the image that you now hold in your hands. Leave it on the altar with your candle burning for 10-15 minutes and visualize yourself sharing that love.

- End this manifesting step by restating your alignment with the Highest Good.

Continue with Steps 7 and 8 when you are done, releasing the circle and recording the ritual.

b) Enjoying Health.

The magickal ritual for health can be a physical one – where we create a sacred space and then engage in a little bit of yoga, stretching or breathing exercises before charging a Red Jasper crystal with the intent to balance and revitalize the physical body. This is my personal favorite as we take care of the mind, body and spirit, while relying on crystal healing to give the physical body an extra boost. The second option would be to make a list of what constitutes good health on all levels, using the automatic writing exercise in Chapter 3, and including all of the ingredients of a healthy and balanced life. Our intuition guides us in creating that list. It might include diet, relationships, meditation, work-life balance, and personal boundaries that we put in place to safeguard our energy levels and stay functional. If you decide to create the written list, be sure to include your full name and date of birth. When I work with crystals, I often use my index finger to inscribe my name on the crystal mentally, rather than scratch it.

End this manifesting step by restating your alignment to the Highest Good, asking your angels and guides to point out any life lessons that may be influencing your experience of health. For more information on why people get sick and how to heal, please read my first book: A Personal Guide to Self-Healing, Cancer & Love. The self-healing and relaxation techniques can be applied to any major illness. The paperback is available on Amazon.

c) Allowing Abundance.

Abundance is about more than money – it includes our experience of love, joy, friendship, inspiration, energy and ambition. While there is such a thing as a magickal free lunch, and we can work magick to generate extra cash on occasion, I find a monthly abundance ritual to be a better strategy. In order to experience abundance on all of those fronts, we need to first release blocks that could keep one or more of those elements beyond our grasp. In this ritual, we ask Archangel Michael to assist with the belief clearing process before creating a crystal spray to attract abundance. To perform this ritual you will need a spray bottle with water, fragments of Citrine and Quartz stones, a label for the bottle, as well as your magickal tools. We will also be connecting with Venus, the planet of love, victory and prosperity. The planets in our solar system have qualities that they can share with us, much like Mother Earth does.

This is the complete clearing and manifesting ritual:

- Ground yourself by visualizing tree roots going out of the bottoms of your feet, into the ground. They wrap around a crystal at the center of the Earth and bring its energy up to your feet and legs. That crystalline energy flows up through your Root, Sacral and Solar Plexus Chakras to your Heart Chakra.

- Take your attention up through the sky, through the atmosphere to a distant star. That star is Venus, the goddess of love, wealth, friendship, and triumph in battles. Her energy is bright gold and green. Connect with her light and bring it back through the atmosphere to your physical body and your Aura.

- This mix of Earth and Venus energies come to mix in your Heart Chakra, combining their life-giving and affluent qualities in one powerful mix. This light ripples out from your Heart, filling your Aura. Take another deep breath and call on Archangel Michael to stand behind you, his hands on your shoulders.

- You are going to begin automatic writing now, asking Michael to point out any limiting beliefs that may block off your experience of abundance. If there is any part of you that feels you do not deserve to be loved, to have money or to life a blissfully happy life, write about those feelings and intend for them to be released from your energy and your unconscious as you continue writing. When that list is full, you are going to visualize it going up in flames. Its energy is sent to the universe for purification.

- Now it is time to create that crystal elixir. We are going to place the pebble-like crystal stones in the small spray bottle. The Citrine pebbles will act as abundance magnets while the Clear Quartz pebbles will continue to clear and release any blocks to abundance in your mind, body or energy. Fill it with water, 3/4th of the way, make sure the crystals are settled in, and hold the spray bottle in your hands.

- Take your attention back to your roots in the ground, the beam of light traveling down from Venus and to Archangel Michael behind you. That energy flows through your body, to your Heart, down your arms to the bottle in your hands. Use your intention to charge this crystal spray with all of these energies: visualize an abundant Earth with ample resources, Venus's wealth, friendship and love and finally Archangel Michael's sword, which continues to shine a light on any blocks, releasing them.

- Visualize yourself filled with abundance, love, friendship, victory, triumph, inspiration and anything else that you could ever need. How would that make you feel – full of freedom and peace of mind. Stay with the feeling and the visualization for 5-10 minutes and when you are done, write your full name on the label along with your date of birth, and the words: clarity, abundance, love, prosperity.

When you are done, restate your alignment with the Highest Good and ask that this harm no one. Release the circle and record the ritual as outlined above. You may want to add a few drops of brandy to the spray bottle to preserve the water – but not too much as you will be spraying this in your Aura. If you would like to add essential oils to the bottle, I would suggest using an orange fruit to stimulate the Sacral Chakra. Over the next few weeks, spray your energy field, your home and your office every day.

We can repeat this every two or three months, always performing the ritual on Friday (Venus day).

An Appeal for Self-Healing

This book is called Chakra Healing & Magick and as you will have noticed, most of the content was focused on healing ourselves by channeling energy, listening to our intuition and working with the Chakras and the Aura creatively, as well as for self-healing. Magick is where we are headed, but we may need to heal ourselves as discussed earlier in this book and explore our full potential before manifesting life-changing opportunities. Otherwise we might not be ready to make the most of a shot when it comes by (although we should be able to manifest another opportunity a few months or years later, when we are ready). To give you a personal example, four years ago I was quitting my job in the corporate world and writing my first book on energy healing. I was determined to make it as a healer and an author, and to facilitate the transition, my managers suggested that I work part time for six months before leaving. To complicate matters just a little bit more, at the time of my quitting, the company planned to transfer me to another job. As a result, I worked one job on Monday, another Tuesday and Wednesday, and then the rest of the week I wrote my book, fit in energy healing sessions and carried on with my Reiki Master training and certification. I couldn't fit anything else on my plate, but my desire to make it as an author manifested something new.

A few weeks into this hectic work schedule, I got a call from an online radio station in the US that was looking for someone to host a weekly show on healing, intuition and oracle cards. My first thought was, *oh my gosh! I would love to do this, but I don't have the time!* And more than that, I was also terrified of hosting a live radio show – what would I say? Would I be able to answer questions? Public speaking was not my thing. At the time, I had a lot of work to do on my Throat Chakra (self-expression) and my Solar

Plexus (confidence). Hosting a radio show would have been completely overwhelming and I politely declined, but I did not leave it there. From then on, I took every "healing" opportunity, volunteering to be a guinea pig in class and putting my fear of public speaking on the table as something to work with.

My Reiki Teacher, a healer by the name of Michael Kaufmann, was incredibly helpful, and one day, that fear just melted away. A few months later I was Automatic Writing in my journal and the message that came through was about giving my voice a platform, a place to be heard. In the next week or so I received emails from three stations, asking if I would like to join as a talk radio host. Eventually, I went back to the station that had contacted me in the beginning, and for the next year and a half, I hosted a show every week. I won't lie; the first few months were nerve wracking but eventually I grew to enjoy taking callers, reading angel and tarot cards live, and speaking about different healing topics. This went on until I felt like I had graduated from *feeling fear* of public speaking to *feeling joy*, and I moved onto new challenges: namely writing for magazines, collaborating as an editor, facilitating workshops and most recently, teaching webinars.

Along the same lines, they say our biggest joy is on the other side of our biggest fear - and with a bit of self-healing and a firm push from our angels and guides, we can cross that bridge and find our bliss.

This wraps up the final chapter on Magickal Co-Creation. If you would like to learn more about how magick empowers us, please subscribe to DiaryofaPsychicHealer.com or to my Regina Chouza YouTube channel for tutorials and meditations. This is a subject that I will continue exploring.

Conclusion

Congratulations for completing this Chakra Healing and Magick workbook! Please pat yourself on the back for completing the course material and practicing the meditations. We have covered a lot of ground in the process. By completing the exercises, you gained the following skills:

- How to ground, clear and shield your personal energy.
- How to heal yourself by exploring the Chakras and the Aura.
- How to run earth energy through the physical body, increasing vitality.
- How to draw on earth and universal energy for self-healing.
- How to send healing to the past, present or future by using a proxy.
- How to activate your energy field and sense your angels and guides.
- How to close down your energy field so that you are not overwhelmed.
- What an angel, a spirit guide and an archangel is.
- How they can help us with different themes in our lives.
- How to connect with your emotions with automatic writing.
- How to connect with our spiritual team in psychic meditations.
- How to plant *intuitive seeds* in your psyche and develop new abilities.
- How to program crystals for Chakra and Aura Healing.
- How to heal yourself with techniques that stimulate all seven Chakras.
- How to work with the tarot for emotional, mental and spiritual healing.
- How to flex your Chakras with meditative prompts and journaling.
- How to work your magick for love, health and abundance.

These tools should keep you busy for a few months or years - it took me three years of studies at *The College of Psychic Studies* and another two the *School of Intuition & Healing* to learn them! The more we practice energy healing and magick, the more powerful our intuitive channel becomes. And of course, self-healing is a continuous process that never ends. I hope you enjoyed this book and I would love to hear from you if you have questions or comments. Self-study is wonderful, but nothing beats signing up for weekly lessons. If you can't find a psychic school or a teacher nearby, I offer online webinars every week, as well as the occasional live stream on metaphysical topics. Please visit my Diary of a Psychic Healer blog for more, and subscribe if you haven't already done so.

I am developing a new technique that involves energy healing, natal astrology and a bit of crystal magick for a completely personalized healing approach. One of the reasons why I published this Chakra Healing & Magick book now was to give us a chance to practice the techniques ahead of the big reveal in 2017-2018. By combining energy healing, crystal magick and natal astrology, we will be able to engage with self-healing on a more profound and personalized level, balancing out personal traits and attitudes that can often hold us back. For example, a person with lots of Water (emotions) and little Earth (grounding) in their chart would be able to capture the energy of the zodiac at a precise moment in time, and take it with them. I can't wait to share it with you! In the meantime, I do include astrology in readings; we can explore healing with the signs and the planets.

Please feel free to reach out if you have any questions, comments or would like to sign up for class! I am also available for psychic readings.

- Email: geena@diaryofapsychichealer.com
- Readings and Classes: www.DiaryofaPsychicHealer.com
- Facebook: www.facebook.com/DiaryofaPsychicHealer
- Video Blog: www.YouTube.com/c/ReginaChouza

Appendix 1
Guided Meditations

Purifying and Relaxing Meditation

Intent: Promote relaxation and harmony in the physical body

Sit down in a quiet and comfortable place. Bring your attention to your breathing and observe its natural pace. As you breathe in, you take in healing energy from the universe. On the out breath, let go of all of the tension in your life. Sit quietly, close your eyes and listen to your breathing.

Take a deep breath in, hold it, and release. Another deep breath in, and release. Let your breath go back to its normal pace, breathing in white light. Breathe out excess energy and waste. As you breathe in, your lungs fill up with life force. As you breathe out, your body lets go of every last toxin. Take another deep breath in, and relax …

Next we will scan the body and let go of any tension from the week.

Start by focusing on your feet and ankles. Are they holding tension? Release and relax. Take your attention to your calves, release any tension and let it fall through the floor.

Moving up your thighs, lower back and hips, continue to release and relax.

Now focus on your abdomen, the digestive system and your other organs. Fill them with purifying white light, and relax. Feel your shoulders, neck and arms. Give them permission to release all tension and stress.

Take another deep breath, hold it and release. Visualize and feel an energy massage going from the top of your head to the soles of your feet.

Bring your attention back to your breathing. Breathe in, then breathe out slowly. Focus on your grounding and bring yourself back to the room.

Aura Cleansing Meditation

Intent: Clear the Aura of any thoughts, stress or tension

Sit in a quiet and comfortable place. Bring your attention to your breathing and observe its natural pace. As you breathe in, you take in healing energy from the universe. As you breathe out, let go of any stress from your life.

Bring your attention to your Heart Chakra, the seat of unconditional love and compassion. As you breathe in, visualize your lungs filling with light.

Next we will work on clearing the Aura:

Visualize a sphere of light around your body. It extends an arm's length in any direction. Sense its color, shape and energy - how does it feel?

See and feel pink and violet light filling the bubble with love. This infusion clears and mobilizes any stagnant energy in your auric field. It flows freely.

Check for any colors or sensations that seem out of place. Send violet light to purify the energy. The light transmutes and releases the energy.

Next, visualize a long grounding cord dropping from your Base Chakra, at the root of your spine, into the ground. This cord lets energy flow down to the center of the Earth where it is cleansed and purified.

Watch from a place of security as gravity sends your worries, cares and concerns to the center of the Earth for purification. Release the cord and let it slip to the center of the Earth as well.

Next we will fill the space left in your Aura with gold. This liquid gold light has the highest vibration of any healing energy. It fills your Aura with the healing power of love and seals it in a protective bubble of gold light.

When your Aura is completely covered, let that gold light trickle down through your Crown Chakra and gently fill your body and your Chakras.

Stay with this image as long as you need to.

When you are ready, bring your attention back to your breath. Feel the weight of the chair under you and slowly bring yourself back to the room.

Chakra Meditation

Intent: Clear, balance and heal the Chakras

Sit down in a comfortable place. Bring your attention to your breathing and observe its natural pace. As you breathe in, you take in healing energy from the universe. As you breathe out, let go of any stress.

Place your hand over the Chakra that you wish to heal. If it is not comfortable to do so, just bring your attention to that part of your body.

Get a sense of how it feels. Do you notice any colors, sensations or intuitive feelings? What do they mean? Let your intuition answer this.

Visualize the Chakra full of light. This light smooths out the edges and dissolves any shadows, patches or colors that you may have noticed.

Next we will fill that Chakra with liquid gold. This liquid gold is unconditional love. It heals the Chakra and raises its vibration to the highest level possible, filling every last inch of space.

Now see and feel the gold rays of light emanating from the Chakra and filling your body, especially the nearby organs and tissues. This gold light purifies, heals and balances the energy in your body. It carries the energy of love. *Sit with this for a few minutes.*

Bring your attention back to the Chakra. This gold healing light starts to fade and instead we find the Chakra full of its natural color.

Use your inner voice to speak to your Chakra, telling it that you will continue to love and care for it. This sends a message to your subconscious, a signal of your commitment to play an active part in your healing process.

When you are ready, bring your attention back to your breath. Feel the weight of the chair under you and bring your attention back to the room. Take all the time you need. When you are ready, open your eyes.

Color Healing Meditation

Intent: Heal and release emotions and energy from the body.

Sit down in a quiet and comfortable place.

Bring your attention to your breathing and observe its natural pace. As you breathe in, you take in healing energy from the universe. On the out breath, let go of all of the tension in your life.

Bring your attention to your Heart Chakra as it fills up with green healing light. This light fills you with comfort, warmth and love. Stay with this throughout the meditation and let your intuition guide you through the rest.

Now bring your attention to your body/Aura/Chakra. How does it feel? Is there a particular area that you would like to heal today? Let your intuition guide you.

Ask your body to show you a color. Go with the first that comes to mind. Is it a solid color? How does it feel like? Is it light, heavy, breezy?

Now ask the color to tell you how it feels. There are no right or wrong answers, everything is valid and deserves to be heard with compassion.

Thank the color for opening up to you. See and feel it filling with white or pink light. This light gently dissolves the color and releases it from your body. Bless it with love and forgiveness.

Next we fill the space with gold liquid. It has the highest vibration of any energy. Visualize it filling any holes and sealing your energy.

Once the space is warm and full of gold, let that gold light trickle down through your Crown Chakra and gently fill your body with gold light.

Bring your attention back to your breath as it settles into its natural rhythm. Feel the weight of the chair beneath you; the soles of your feet. Take your time and slowly bring your attention to the room.

When you are ready open your eyes.

Meet Your Magickal Guide (Clairvoyant Meditation)

Intent: Psychic Meditation to Meet Your Guide

My favorite meditations are what you might call psychic journeys, where we bring our brain waves down to a semi-hypnotic level and let our intuition speak to us. To do these safely we start by grounding and protecting our energy. You will find a similar "Inner Child" meditation on my YouTube.

Close your eyes, take a few deep breaths and visualize the room around you. It is suddenly filled with white light from above – this light clears the room of any unnecessary energy, creating a clear and safe space for you to connect with your guides. This light creates a shield, only the purest and highest vibrational beings are able to enter this sacred space.

Ground yourself by visualizing tree roots growing out of the bottoms of your feet, into the ground. These roots wrap around an Amethyst crystal in the center of the Earth, drawing on its violet energy to activate your intuition. See and feel that energy as it rises to meet you.

That crystalline energy continues to flow up, through your feet, your calves and your thighs to the Root Chakra at the base of your spine. This red disc overflows with energy, and the light continues to rise through your Sacral Chakra in the lower abdomen and the Solar Plexus, under your Heart. The light comes to rest in your Heart Chakra. Stay here for a moment, watching these four chakras spin brightly, red, orange, yellow and pinkish green.

Take your attention up through the ceiling and the sky, to the source of that white light. You thank that light for clearing and shielding your personal space, and ask that it now activate your intuition. Follow that beam of light to your Crown Chakra, and see and feel this violet Chakra as it opens up to receive that light. You may feel prickly sensations on your scalp.

That light flows down your core, through your Brow and Throat Chakras, which also shine brightly and expand. See and feel these energy centers growing stronger, front and back.

The light comes to rest in your Heart Chakra, which is now overflowing with earth and sky energies. Feel it expand, and ask your guardian angel to take his place behind you. Your angel is going to raise your vibration so that you can see and feel your guides clearly.

Now the Journey Begins

Visualize a door in front of you. How big is it? What color and what material? How easily are you able to open the door? When you are ready, step through it and let you guardian angel follow you into your own personal Neverland.

We now step into a hallway. To your right is a staircase leading down. As you approach the staircase pay attention to your surroundings. Take a step down the stairs, moving slowly while you focus on your breath. We count down with each step: 10, 9, 8, 7, 6, 5, 3, 2, 1.

We reach the bottom and find a swimming pool. You dive in and swim to the other side, your body sliding through the water safely and easily. A towel materializes in front of you; pat yourself dry before moving on.

At the end of the hall we see a tree trunk with a hollow center. You climb up the inside of the tree trunk easily, fully supported by the tree. It takes you up, to a magickal place full of flowers, animals and even a few mythical creatures.

One of these creatures approaches you with a flower. This mystical creature is your guide. Ask their name. They are here to help you reconnect with that childish sense of wonder.

Look at the flower and bring it close to your Heart, which now opens up to receive its messages. Your physical eyes are closed, but your Heart's eye is wide open, and listening.

The creature asks you to climb on it's back, so that it can take you on a journey through the park. Keep your intuitive eyes and ears open, making a note of any sights or sounds.

Give yourself a few minutes in silence to enjoy the journey.

Closing Down

When the tour is done, you come back to the tree. You thank them for the message. Make your way back down the tree, through the swimming pool and up the stairs to your magickal door. Step through the door, closing it gently behind you. You can return anytime you like.

Bring your attention back to your grounding roots and the violet bubble of light. When you are ready, open your eyes and make a note of everything you sensed.

Note: The sights, sounds, colors and textures all carry a message. Think about how you felt as you made your way through the door. Were you refreshed by the pool? How did the child communicate with you? Take 5-10 minutes to write about the experience. This is when the messages usually start to click. If there was anything that you didn't understand, make a note of it because the significance may be clearer in time.

Appendix 2
Chakra Quiz Follow Up

In this section you will find a little bit of information on the chakra quizzes in Chapter 4. There are no right or wrong answers – the idea is to identify how you feel and how you would respond in situations that would be related to each of the Chakras. Below you will find a brief explanation for the composition of the quiz. The general rule is that anything that pushes our buttons can be healed and released; the annoyance is a message in itself.

Root Chakra Quiz

The questions included are about how safe and comfortable we feel in our physical bodies, with an eye to the experiences we may have had as children (or before we were born). As the Root Chakra is also linked to our grounding and presence in the world, I have included a few questions about our bearings and how self-aware we are (car keys and wallet). Finally, how we feel about the color red can be indicative of this Chakra, though it is possible to associate other themes with this color.

Sacral Chakra Quiz

The questions included in this section are about our creativity on both a aesthetic level, and how creative we are spiritually and magickally; are we are aware of the moon's cycles and how we can work with them to manifest changes in our lives? After all, this is the Chakra that takes the wisdom and intuition from our so-called spiritual Chakras, and channels it into the physical world around us. It also rules our emotions, including how aware we are of our own feelings and those of others. There are a few questions on movies such as *Jumanji* or *Hook*, all in reference to our inner child.

Solar Plexus Chakra Quiz

The questions in this section are about personal power, confidence, boundaries and how beliefs and experiences shape the roles we play in life. For example, do we play the victim, the savior? Were you the popular kid in high school or the math geek turned millionaire? Some of these labels are figments of our imagination (ego), others are embedded in our personality. The questions in the Solar Plexus Chakra section are about who we are on a "human" vs. "spiritual" level, and how our experience of personal power can vary with the role that we choose to play. These roles can be questioned and erased, if we work with the Solar Plexus (personal identity) and the Brow Chakras (beliefs, concepts).

Heart Chakra Quiz

The questions in this section are about how we balance giving and receiving in our lives. The first question uses a visual prompt to assess the energetic strength our giving and receiving sides. Ideally both flowers would be equal in size, shape and color – with only minor differences. The Heart Chakra rules our experience of love and abundance, as we receive with this energy center. If it is too wide open, we sometimes risk accepting unhealthy treatment from others. If it is on the narrow side, we may be keeping out an experience that could be wonderful, such as love or abundance. Finally, as the center of unconditional love, it also influences our ability to love and honor ourselves.

Throat Chakra Quiz

The questions in this section are about communication, honesty, and self-expression. It also asks us to explore the concept of Truth from two energetic sources. We have one "truth" in our Hearts and this is influenced by our intuition and sense of compassion. We may have another "truth" in the Brow Chakra, and this one can be influenced by false beliefs or judgments that color our view of the world. If the Throat is speaking the Brow's truth, are we tapping into "beliefs and biases" or are we able to detach ourselves and look at the big picture? These questions also ask us to consider how empowered and vocal we are, shouting "shotgun" when opportunity knocks, or taking a back seat.

Brow Chakra Quiz

The questions in this section are about our ability to pierce the filters created by our personal beliefs. Are we able to see the world objectively? Are our thoughts tinged by false beliefs or judgments? To some extent we all carry beliefs, the question is how do these shape our experiences. As the seat of the Third Eye, Brow Chakra quiz also includes questions on mental creativity and visualization. If for example, we find it hard to read a book and see its world in our mind's eye, it may take a little bit longer for clairvoyance to develop. But we can rely on the other psychic skills so that is not a problem.

Crown Chakra Quiz

The questions in this section are about the strength of our connection to divine love and intelligence. As I have seen with numerous healing clients, that connection can be very strong even if we do not see ourselves as particularly intuitive or psychic. It is about our connection to that part of us that is eternal, as the Crown Chakra communicates with our higher self. The questions focus largely on our sense of direction in life, and our self-belief. When this Chakra opens up and receives divine energy, which then flows to the rest of our Chakras, we discover our true potential and power.

Appendix 3
Suggested Reading List

Schools for Healing and Intuition

- www.youtube.com/c/ReginaChouza (Coming Soon!)
- http://www.intuitionandhealing.co.uk/(UK)
- http://www.collegeofpsychicstudies.co.uk/(UK)
- http://www.barbarabrennan.com/(US & Austria)
- http://www.reiki-meditation.co.uk(UK)

Books on Energy Healing and Chakras

- *The Aura and the Chakras an Owner's Manual* by Karla McLaren
- *The Seven Lies of the Human Race*, by Maria Veiga
- *The Essence of Self-Healing* by Petrene Soames
- *Anatomy of the Spirit* by Caroline Myss

Books on Angels and Psychic Development

- *Ask Your Guides* by Sonia Choquette
- *Psychic Development Simplified* by "Nathaniel" Usarzewicz
- *Tarot: Learn How to Read and Interpret the Cards* by Kim Arnold
- *The Mythic Tarot* by Juliet Sharman-Burke and Liz Greene

Books on Magick

- *Sane Occultism* by Dion Fortune
- *Practical Magick for Beginners* by Brandy Williams
- *Wicca Crystal Magick* by Lisa Chamberlain
- *Ascension Magic* by Christopher Penczack
- *Modern Magic: 12 Lessons in High Magic*, by Donald M. Kraig

Appendix 4
Glossary Of Terms

The Angels and the Archangels are beings of light that serve, protect and guide us. We each have a Guardian Angel by our side as well as a team of archangels who are happy to assist us individually and collectively.

The Aura is the energy field surrounding the human body. All of our thoughts, emotions, feelings and reactions are stored in the Aura.

The Brow Chakra is the energy center at the forehead. The Brow is linked to our thinking capabilities, analytical skills and intuitive vision. Related organs: eyes and brain. Its color, indigo.

The Chakras are our personal energy centers. They regulate the flow of energy in the physical, emotional, mental and spiritual body. Each of the major Chakras relates to a specific area in our life: spirituality, sight, communication, love, power, relationships and security.

The Crown Chakra is the energy center situated at the crown of the head. A clear Crown enables us to receive intuitive messages and guidance. Related organs: brain, eyes, central nervous system. Its color, violet.

Crystal Healing involves working with crystalline structures to clear, balance, heal or shield our personal energy. Different crystals are suitable for different purposes, Chakras, Aura layers, etc.

Channeling is the process of drawing on universal healing energy and sharing it with others. Healers channel energy through their Heart Chakras.

Clairaudience is one of the seven psychic abilities. It is when we receive messages as sounds, words, music lyrics or as an inner voice that speaks to us. It is governed by the Throat Chakra.

Clairsentience is one of the seven psychic abilities. It's when we feel physical sensations, such as a pang in the stomach or the presence of your angels behind you. It is ruled by the Root Chakra.

Clairvoyance is the psychic ability known as vision. We may see images, symbols, photos, faces or even words in our mind's eye. It also enables us to see life clearly. It is ruled by the Third Eye.

Energy clearing is when we work with earth or universal energies to clear remove energy from a space where it does not belong, whether it is a human being's Aura, home or work space.

Energy Healing is a complementary therapy that involves clearing and healing imbalances on the physical, emotional, mental and spiritual levels.

Energetic Protection (Shielding) is the practice of using universal and earth energies to insulate ourselves from psychic, energetic or emotional phenomena. It desensitizes the energy body. .

A Healer is a person who channels healing energy. There are natural healers who are able to channel energy with minimal training, as well as qualified healers who study energy healing for months or even years.

The Healee is the person who receives energy healing in a hands-on or distant healing session.

The Heart Chakra is the energy center that enables us to give and receive love. We can send healing to any organ through the Heart. Related organs: heart, cardiovascular system, lungs, immune system and breast. Its color, green or pink.

Intuition is often defined as the ability to know something without proof. Commonly referred to as our sixth sense, we have seven psychic abilities and this "inner knowing" is only one of them.

Grounding is the practice of anchoring ourselves in the Earth's energy so that we can live present lives, fully engaged with the human experience. It provides an escape valve for excess energy and emotions, as well as the support and foundations of Mother Earth to build upon.

Guided Visualizations are relaxation techniques that involve mentally seeing and feeling a sequence of events. For example: "Visualize yourself walking by the beach. Listen to the waves. Feel the sand under you toes."

Magic with a "C" refers to stage magic – bunnies being pulled out of hats to please a crowd.

Magick with a "CK" refers to the spiritual practice that aims to create a change in the magician, and often a change in the world with which they interact, through rituals,

Meditation involves focusing the mind on a thought, idea or concept. This can include observing the breath, repeating a mantra or bringing your attention to a particular concept, object (e.g., a candle) or a mental picture.

The Mind's Eye is the mental faculty that makes it possible for us to picture an image in our mind, as you would if you were to go to the movies and recall a funny scene the next evening.

Psychic Development is the process of engaging with the energy body – the Aura and the Chakras – in meditation to develop the seven psychic skills and access our intuition everyday.

The Root Chakra is located at the base of the spine. It relates to our feelings of vitality, safety and community. It is also linked to the physical Aura layer. Related organs: skeleton, skin and bowels. Its color, red.

The Sacral Chakra is the energy center below the navel. It is linked to our creative drive, passion and our relationships. Related organs: bladder, kidneys and female reproductive organs. Its color, orange.

Shielding is a technique that desensitizes our energy and protects it from the psychic and energetic realms. We can shield ourselves quickly by visualizing violet light around our body.

The Solar Plexus Chakra is the energy center in upper stomach. It is the seat of our personal power and reflects self-esteem. Related organs: stomach, liver, spleen, and digestive system. Its color, yellow.

Spirit Guides are beings who for the most part, led human existences and excelled in one area of their life, such as work, family life, science, spirituality, technology, etc. They coach us from the other side, and often without our being aware of their presence. We can reach out to them directly, once we have learned to open up safely and communicate.

The Throat Chakra governs our ability to communicate our thoughts, feelings and emotions. Related organs: throat, ears, thyroid, esophagus and neck. Its color, light blue.

ABOUT THE AUTHOR

Can anyone learn to channel healing and shift his or her life in a new direction? Absolutely! This startling discovery led Regina Chouza to become an Accredited Healer, blogger and teacher. Her first book, *A Personal Guide to Self-Healing, Cancer & Love* is also available on Amazon. She teaches intuition workshops in Mexico City, as well as online through a new partnership with OM Times Magazine. Regina is a qualified Healer with the School of Intuition & Healing, UK. She also studied psychic development for more than three years at The College of Psychic Studies. Please visit DiaryofaPsychicHealer.com to subscribe to the blog, or to book a reading.